At Issue

Gerrymandering and Voting Districts

Other Books in the At Issue Series

At Issue

Gerrymandering and Voting Districts

Rita Santos, Book Editor

GREENHAVEN
PUBLISHING

Published in 2019 by Greenhaven Publishing, LLC
353 3rd Avenue, Suite 255, New York, NY 10010

Cover image: John David Bigl III/Shutterstock.com

Cataloging-in-Publication Data

Names: Santos, Rita, editor.
Title: Gerrymandering and voting districts / edited by Rita Santos.
Description: New York : Greenhaven Publishing, 2019. | Series: At issue | Includes
  bibliographical references and index. | Audience: Grades 9–12.
Identifiers: LCCN ISBN 9781534503250 (library bound) | ISBN 9781534503267 (pbk.)
Subjects: LCSH: Gerrymandering—United States. | Apportionment (Election law)—
  United States. | Election districts—United States. | Voting—United States.
Classification: LCC JK1341.G477 2019 | DDC 328.73/073455—dc23

Manufactured in the United States of America

Website: http://greenhavenpublishing.com

Contents

Introduction

The 2012 election was the first since 1972 in which the political party that won the most votes did not win the most congressional seats. This trend would continue through the 2016 presidential election, when Hillary Clinton received nearly 3 million more votes than her opponent but still did not win the election. Although there are many theories about what exactly contributed to Donald Trump's victory, some claim that a political trick called gerrymandering was among them. While the term and the practice have been around since 1812, most Americans, besides politicians, have likely heard it only in passing. Given the huge impact gerrymandering has on American democracy, it deserves more attention.

Every state has a different number of elected members of Congress based on its population. These representatives are chosen to represent different portions of the state called districts. Because people move to new places of residence and the population of towns can change, districts are redrawn every few years. Many state constitutions allow politicians to draw district lines. When these lines are drawn in a way that intentionally makes it more likely that one party or candidate will win, it's referred to as gerrymandering. This happens less often in states that do not allow politicians to draw district lines. Gerrymandering effectively rigs the electoral system so that a particular side is almost guaranteed to win. While it doesn't force anyone to change their vote, it does intentionally weaken the power of a specific group of people's vote. This creates elections that are unfair and undemocratic: all votes are not truly equal.

The goal of gerrymandering is to make the votes of one political party count for more than the votes of people from another party. This is usually done by a method known as "cracking," in which districts are drawn so that voters of one party are spread out into several districts. The alternative approach is called "packing," which takes place when one party's voters are "packed" into one district. It's common to find examples of both cracking and packing in the same state. To achieve the goal of either cracking or packing a district, politicians will sometimes draw district borders that make little or no geographic sense.

However, there are some who think gerrymandering can serve a useful purpose in particular contexts. The Voting Rights Act of 1965 prohibited drawing district lines that diminished the power of people of color to elect representatives. Some districts use gerrymandering to either remedy or avoid violating the Voting Rights Act. In order to ensure that the votes of people of color matter, some states choose to pack minority voters into one district. This type of gerrymandering is referred to as a "majority-minority district." The legality of this type of gerrymandering has been tested in several court cases, such as *Shaw v. Reno* and *Cooper v. Harris*, which are further explored in this text. So far, courts have upheld racial gerrymandering as long as it's done to protect minority voters. Many people support majority-minority districts, as they believe they are a useful strategy to guarantee more people of color are elected to office. Others, like viewpoint author Richard Valelly and the nonprofit FairVote, think that packing minorities into (usually) one district is a form of racial segregation. In this collection, FairVote will explain the assertion that these districts actually dilute the power of minority votes. By packing minorities into a single district it means other state representatives have less incentive to listen to minority voters. Gerrymandering is always good for one side. When it comes to majority-minority districts, it can sometimes be hard to say which side comes out on top.

When politicians don't have to worry about winning an election, they have nothing to compel them to follow the will of the people. In a fair election, if constituents didn't like the performance of their incumbent representative, they could elect someone else. In this scenario, the politician has a clear incentive to make his constituents happy. When gerrymandering occurs, however, the constituents that politicians actually need to please are the ones they have selected for themselves. Even if the majority of the politician's constituents don't vote to reelect them, the politician still wins. A gerrymandered system is much easier for politicians to manipulate and much worse for the people they represent.

One of the most significant issues when it comes to fighting gerrymandering is that the Supreme Court has refused to provide a clear standard for measuring it. This makes legal battles to prove that gerrymandering is taking place very hard to win. The upcoming Supreme Court trial *Gill v. Whitford* will offer the court another chance to give a legal standard to what exactly constitutes illegal gerrymandering. The ruling could have possible effects on redistricting for the 2020 presidential election.

Gerrymandering isn't a sign that a particular political party is corrupt: it's a flaw in our system that both major parties attempt to exploit to some degree. However, it is still a flaw that must be eliminated. In this collection, readers will be introduced to perspectives on gerrymandering from viewpoint authors such as Kristin Eberhard, Matthew Spector, and Brenda Wright, who have all proposed various solutions to prevent gerrymandering. Others have suggested using algorithms based on the state's shape, population, and number of districts. However, one of the easiest ways to avoid the issue entirely is to take politicians out of the mix when drawing districts. Countries like the United Kingdom have found great success in having independent third parties draw district lines instead of politicians. Occasionally, the third parties are also denied access to certain information like the voter records or population demographics to ensure non-biased redistricting. Using independent third parties has proven to be one of the most successful ways to solve the problem. Unfortunately, decisions about who will take part in redistricting decisions are still legally in the hands of politicians. It is against politicians' self-interests to prevent gerrymandering, so it is up to citizens to demand the use of independent third parties.

The viewpoints in *At Issue: Gerrymandering and Voting Districts* will take an in-depth look at the history and effects of gerrymandering in America. They will provide a deeper understanding of how exactly gerrymandering works and discuss the proposed methods to prevent it—because democracies work better when voters choose their politicians, not the other way around.

What Is Gerrymandering and How Does It Affect Voters?

Liz Kennedy, Billy Corriher, and Danielle Root

Liz Kennedy is the director of democracy and government reform at American Progress. Billy Corriher is the deputy director of legal progress at American Progress, where his work focuses on courts, the law, and the influence of judicial elections and campaign contributions on judges. Danielle Root is the voting rights manager for democracy and government at American Progress.

The Center for American Progress is a nonpartisan think tank that strives to improve the lives of all Americans through proposing new policy measures. One of the issues it is raising awareness about is gerrymandering. As the viewpoint authors will explain, the organization asserts that gerrymandering creates an electoral process that is free of electoral choice and healthy competition between politicians. They also fear that it makes politicians harder to hold accountable for their actions. They have come up with a three-step process that could make voting more democratic. The authors are hopeful that by working together Americans can solve the problem of gerrymandering.

When voters cast a ballot, they expect their votes to matter in choosing representatives who are responsive, reflective, and

This material, "Redistricting and Representation" by Liz Kennedy, Billy Corriher, and Danielle Root, was created by the Center for American Progress, https://www.americanprogress.org/issues/democracy/reports/2016/12/05/294272/redistricting-and-representation/, Reprinted by permission.

accountable to the communities they represent. Election districts for federal, state, and local offices should be drawn to advance those ends. Unfortunately, politicians in many states have manipulated election districts to choose their voters, rather than having voters choose them.[1]

Electoral maps must follow the principle of "one person, one vote," in which each district has a substantially similar number of people. But in most states, legislators can draw election districts in ways that manipulate the map for their own interests—called gerrymandering. For example, gerrymandering can tilt the playing field in favor of the politicians or party in power.[2] Allowing politicians to draw their own election districts without checks and balances is like letting the fox guard the henhouse.

When elected officials are given exclusive, unfettered power to manipulate district lines, voters lose. Members of the US House of Representatives are re-elected 97 percent of the time.[3] And in the 2016 election, only 10 percent of the 435 House seats were considered competitive.[4] In addition to creating an electoral process largely free of electoral choice and healthy competition, gerrymandering can insulate politicians from accountability and block communities from receiving meaningful and fair representation. In 2012, Democrats in the US House of Representatives received 1.4 million more votes than Republicans, but Republicans won the majority of seats.[5] That election marked the first time since 1972 that the party with the most votes did not get the most seats in Congress.[6] Advances in technology have exacerbated the problem of gerrymandering by making it easier for map drawers to identify neighborhood demographics and voter preferences. Politicians are able to use this technology to slice and dice voters into districts along partisan and racial lines more precisely than ever before.[7]

Americans are taking matters into their own hands by advancing redistricting reforms to revitalize their elected representation and by filing lawsuits challenging corrupted district maps. People are winning victories for policy reforms, such as the recent success in California, where voters passed an initiative to set up an independent redistricting commission.[8] Legal challenges to improperly drawn maps continue to move through the courts. Since 2010, 224 lawsuits challenging district lines have been filed across the country, 32 of which are still active.[9] In November 2016, a federal court in Wisconsin struck down the state's 2011 state assembly district maps as unconstitutional, marking the first time a state legislative redistricting plan was ruled unconstitutional for partisan gerrymandering.[10] The court there found that Republicans had manipulated the state's legislative boundaries for partisan advantage. Also in November 2016, a federal court ordered North Carolina lawmakers to redraw their state legislative districts after finding that lawmakers unconstitutionally relied on race when drawing district boundaries.[11] On December 5, the US Supreme Court will hear oral arguments in two redistricting cases involving challenges to districts in Virginia and North Carolina.

Some states are not waiting around for a court ruling to make their redistricting processes fairer and more representative. Several states have established independent redistricting commissions, and Florida incorporated clear criteria governing the process of drawing districts into its state constitution.

Americans are tired of having their voting power and representation manipulated by politicians who draw district maps to further their own interests. If citizens want elected representatives who reflect their priorities and preferences, they must push for reforms that will result in fair boundaries for election districts. The Center for American Progress recommends that states:

- Establish independent redistricting commissions
- Ensure clear redistricting criteria
- Promote public input and transparency in their redistricting processes

By putting these mechanisms in place, reflective and responsive representation may be fully realized and enjoyed by all Americans.

Gerrymandering Hurts Voters

When district lines are manipulated, the democratic process is turned on its head. Voters may not be able to elect who they want, while map drawers are able to skew election results to favor themselves. And when politicians are guaranteed to win because gerrymandering has effectively precluded competitive elections, it diminishes responsiveness, accountability, and the potential for fair representation of all their constituents.

Representational Mismatch

Redistricting can skew representation. In Pennsylvania in 2012, Democratic candidates received roughly 50 percent of the votes in House races, but Republicans took 75 percent of congressional seats.[16] The same thing occurred in North Carolina, where Democrats received more than half of all votes, but Republicans claimed 70 percent of congressional seats.[17] In Michigan too, despite Democratic candidates winning the most votes in 2012, Republicans took the majority of seats.[18] Voters in Michigan experienced the same thing again in 2014, when Republicans retained congressional control despite Democratic candidates receiving the majority of votes.[19] In Maryland in 2014, Democratic candidates received 57 percent of the vote but won seven out of eight House seats.[20]

On the state level, despite Democrats in Ohio winning more than 50 percent of the popular vote cast for the state legislature in 2012, Democratic members held just 39 of 99 seats in the wake of that election.[21] In five other state legislatures, people cast more votes for candidates from one of the major parties, but the other party still controlled the state legislature.[22]

This mismatched pattern continued through this year's election cycle in places such as Pennsylvania, Wisconsin, and repeat offender Michigan. In Pennsylvania, voters cast ballots for Democrats and Republicans in near equal numbers, yet 13 of the state's 18 congressional seats went to Republicans.[23] In Wisconsin, votes cast for Democratic and Republican candidates in statewide races were split roughly 50-50, but thanks to the GOP's district manipulations, Republicans won control of nearly two-thirds of the legislature.[24] And just as in 2012 and 2014, voters in Michigan saw Republicans retain control of the legislature, even though Democratic candidates once again received the majority of votes.

Noncompetitive Elections

When politicians manipulate election maps, they can stifle competition and ensure incumbent candidates keep their seats. Because of gerrymandering, the political majorities of the incoming state legislatures in eight states were already decided before even a single vote was cast in the 2016 general election, while seven state legislature majorities were decided even before the primary election.[25] In those places, district lines were drawn to ensure that only one major party candidate was viable to run in uncontested races.[26] Only 4 percent of districts nationwide were decided by five percentage points or less, while only eight percent were decided by 10 points or less.[27] Ninety-two percent of elections for seats in the House of Representatives were decided by a margin of victory exceeding 10 points.[28]

Policy Outcome Mismatch

The manipulation of election districts also has broader effects on the health of states' democracy, according to a 2015 Center for American Progress Action Fund report.[29] It "creates an echo chamber in which candidates and elected officials are responsible only to people of like demography and ideology, rather than to a broad base of voters."[30]

As a result, they are able to pass laws that are averse to the interests and desires of those they represent. For example, in Michigan, where elected leaders have a long history of manipulating district lines, controversial legislation has been funneled through the state legislature, despite vehement opposition from voters.[31] For example, "over a clear majority of residents' objections," Michigan lawmakers passed a controversial "rape insurance" law in 2014 and the state's Religious Freedom

Restoration Act in 2015.[32] Only 36 percent of Michigan voters supported the rape insurance law, which required women to purchase a separate insurance policy for any future nonemergency abortion procedure.[33]Moreover, 70 percent of Michigan voters wanted marriage equality protections expanded in 2015.[34] This is in contrast to the state's Religious Freedom Restoration Act, which allowed adoption agencies to deny service to same-sex couples.[35] In 2012, Michigan voters rejected the state's emergency manager legislation through referendum, legislation that would have allowed the state to strip locally elected governments of their power.[36] However, elected officials ultimately ignored the clear wishes of their constituents a year later, when they passed the law and used the authority to strip the municipal governments of Flint and other cities of their authority.[37] Unfortunately, because of the state's manipulated district maps, Michigan voters did not have any realistic opportunity to vote these representatives out of office.

[...]

Recommendations for Drawing Fairer Election Districts

To address the manipulation of maps by politicians, voters must look beyond the courtroom and demand reforms that take these decisions out of the hands of politicians. At the very least, the redistricting process must include proper constraints and clear guidance, as well as public transparency and input. Some states have set up processes that minimize the power of politicians to manipulate the districts, including establishing independent redistricting commissions, creating clear legal guidelines for drawing district maps, and opening the process up to the public.

Establish Independent Redistricting Commissions

Several Western states use independent commissions to draw election districts using fair, neutral criteria.[38] Most of these states have transparent processes, rather than politicians who operate behind closed doors.

States and local jurisdictions should follow the lead of California and establish bipartisan independent redistricting commissions responsible for drawing congressional and local district maps. Independent commissions offer several benefits, including eliminating the appearance of impropriety and making elections fairer. Legislators, for instance, are four times more likely than independent commissions to create congressional districts that "deny voters choices in the primary" and two times more likely to do so for general elections.[39] This is perhaps one of the reasons why maps drawn by independent commissions face fewer legal challenges than maps drawn by politicians.[40]

There are different ways to design independent or citizen-led redistricting commissions. These commissions should be comprised of an equal number of members associated with each major party, ensuring that at least one member from the opposing party must vote for any plan before it is implemented.[41] Missouri and Idaho, for example, require that an even number of commissioners are appointed from each party. Missouri goes so far to require a supermajority to approve any final redistricting plan to ensure that all views are considered.[42] Alternatively, an independent commission could be comprised of an equal number of members from each major party, plus one tiebreaker who is appointed by the judiciary and not registered with either of the major parties.[43]

In addition to partisan diversity, members of any independent commission should be representative of demographic differences to ensure that the commission is representative of the populations in the districts it is responsible for drawing. Jurisdictions may require that one or more commissioners be chosen from each region, while others may require that a commission "reflect the racial, ethnic, geographic, and gender diversity of the state."[44]

In California,[45] a panel of state auditors chooses 20 potential commissioners—with an even number of Republicans, Democrats, and independents.[46] Legislators from both parties can each remove two of the 20 names.[47] Of the remaining 16, the first eight commissioners are chosen at random, though it must include three Democrats, three Republicans, and two independents.[48] The eight commissioners then appoint the remaining six, with equal numbers from all three groups.[49] A district map must be approved by nine of the commission's 14 members, and the approving members must include three members from both parties and three independent members.[50] The maps can even be overturned by voters.[51]

At the local level in California, Sacramento and Berkeley residents recently approved ballot measures that establish independent redistricting commissions for drawing local city council maps beginning after the 2020 Census.[52] The new Sacramento Independent Redistricting Commission will be composed of 13 members, "one from each of the eight council districts, picked by a screening panel and the other five by the chosen eight."[53] The panel will have exclusive power to draw district lines.[54] Similar to Sacramento, Berkeley's new independent commission will be comprised of 13 members, all of whom must apply for the position and must be registered city voters.[55] The city clerk will select members every 10 years after each new census.[56] In order to protect the commission's independence, current and former city council members are prohibited from serving. Both measures are aimed at taking map-drawing power out of the hands of those who are elected through them.[57]

Arizona voters also approved a state constitutional amendment to take authority over drawing districts from politicians and put it into the hands of an independent, bipartisan commission.[58] Arizona politicians sued to have the amendment overturned, but the US Supreme Court rejected their argument.[59] Justice Ruth Bader Ginsburg's opinion discussed the history of the amendment and noted, "Redistricting plans adopted by the Arizona Legislature sparked controversy in every redistricting cycle since the 1970's."[60] Justice Ginsburg also noted studies showing that "nonpartisan and bipartisan commissions generally draw their maps in a timely fashion and create districts both more competitive and more likely to survive legal challenge."[61]

Ensure Clear Redistricting Criteria

If elected officials are tasked with drawing district lines, there must be clear criteria by which they must abide. These criteria should be established under law either through individual redistricting statutes or by including them in the state constitution, as was done in Florida. They must set out the basic principles of redistricting, namely creating fair and neutral district schemes by prohibiting manipulation to achieve partisan goals. The criteria should include barring consideration of party affiliation and voting records and maintaining communities of interest and neighborhoods when possible. By doing so, much of the improper political maneuvering can be taken out of the process. In addition, there should be a clear standard against which voters can hold elected official accountable for the maps that they draw.

Some state constitutions also outline the criteria that legislators must follow when drawing election districts.[62] Most constitutions require that districts be compact and try to respect political boundaries, such as counties and cities.[63] Other state constitutions have been amended to prohibit partisan goals or to require neutral, fair criteria for drawing maps.[64]

The Florida Constitution, for example, was amended to say that districts "may not be drawn to favor or disfavor an incumbent or political party."[65] The Florida Supreme Court ruled in 2015 that the state legislature's 2011 map violated this requirement, and it noted that legislators drew the maps in a secret process to maximize benefit to the legislature's Republican majority:

> The Legislature itself proclaimed that it would conduct the most open and transparent redistricting process in the history of the state, and then made important decisions, affecting numerous districts in the enacted map, outside the purview of public scrutiny.[66]

The court ruled that "the redistricting process and resulting map were taint[ed] by unconstitutional intent to favor the Republican Party and incumbents" and ordered a new map.[67]

Require Transparency and Public Input

Regardless of whether a jurisdiction's maps are drawn by an independent commission or by elected officials, transparency and public input is important. The public should be an integral part of the process—for example, through public hearings on proposed district plans or by allowing voters to submit their own proposed plans. At minimum, proposed maps should be published online and in local newspapers for the public to review and analyze prior to implementation. Those responsible for drawing district maps may also be required to justify, on the record, the reasons they drew the lines in the way that they did.[68] While most members of the public are not experts in the process of redistricting, they are perhaps best positioned to "know more about the effect of certain district configurations on local communities than legislators or commissioners" as they are the ones most directly affected by such plans.[69]

Of course, allowing opportunity for public comment and public hearings over proposed maps requires additional time that would perhaps not otherwise be needed if maps were simply pushed through the legislature by a controlling party. However, allowing such participation is important and necessary in ensuring that redistricting maps are fair and fully representative of the people they encompass.

Conclusion

In many places, elected officials are still in charge of drawing the electoral maps that get them elected. These officials should have the best interests of voters in mind when they draw district maps. But much of the time, elected officials are more interested in making sure they get re-elected or that their party remains in power, often at the expense of voter preferences.

Reform is needed in the redistricting process. Current cases being heard by the Supreme Court may help lead the way by more clearly defining what drawers of district maps can take into account when creating them and to what extent. At the state and local level, however, jurisdictions must act to make the redistricting process fairer and more transparent. They can start by establishing independent redistricting commissions or by passing laws that clearly establish criteria and rules that map drawers must abide by in creating district maps. Jurisdictions must also open the process up to the public and encourage public input and participation. In this way, voters can receive the fair representation to which they are entitled.

Endnotes

1. Elizabeth Kolbert, "Drawing the Line," *The New Yorker*, June 27, 2016.

2. Ibid.

3. Open Secrets, "Reelection Rates Over the Years," available at https://www .opensecrets.org/overview/reelect.php (last accessed November 2016).

4. Lisa Mascaro, "Gerrymandering helped Republicans take control of Congress, but now it's tearing them apart over Trump," *Los Angeles Times*, October 11, 2016.

5. John Harwood, "Democrats Make Advances, but House Still Proves Elusive," *The New York Times*, July 5, 2015.

6. Scott Keyes, "Republicans Brag They Won the House Majority Because of Gerrymandering," ThinkProgress, January 17, 2013.

7. Julian E. Zelizer, "The power that gerrymandering has brought to Republicans," *The Washington Post*, June 17, 2016.

8. Common Cause, "California Voters Pass Sweeping Democracy Reform," Press release, November 9, 2016.

9. Justin Levitt, "Litigation in the 2010 Cycle," All About Redistricting. In at least 13 of those cases, states were ordered to redraw their districts. Ballotpedia, "Redistricting lawsuits related to the 2010 Census."

10. The Campaign Legal Center, "Historic Decision: Wisconsin Federal Court Strikes Down Partisan Gerrymander and Adopts Groundbreaking Legal Standard," Press release, November 21, 2016.

11. Mark Binker, "Federal court orders new NC legislative elections in 2017," WRAL, November 29, 2016, available at http://www.wral.com/federal-court-orders-new-nc -legislative-elections-in-2017/16289906/; *Covington v. North Carolina*, No. 1:15-CV-399 (M.D.N.C. Nov. 29, 2016). The court set a deadline of March 15, 2017, for new maps to be drawn and required the state to hold new elections by the end of next year.

12. Iowa Code §§ 42.3, 42.5, available at https://coolice.legis.iowa.gov/Cool-ICE/default .asp?category=billinfo&service=IowaCode&ga=83&input=42. See also, Justin Levitt, "A Citizens Guide to Redistricting" (New York: Brennan Center for Justice, 2010), available at https://www.brennancenter.org/sites/default/files/legacy/CGR%20 Reprint%20Single%20Page.pdf.

13. *Wesberry v. Sanders*, 376 U.S. 1 (1964).

14. 52 U.S. Code § 10301.

15. See generally, *Brown v. Detzner*, Case No. 4:15cv398-MW/CAS (N.D.FL).

16. Adam Serwer and others, "Now That's What I Call Gerrymandering!" *Mother Jones*, November 14, 2012, available at http://www.motherjones.com/politics/2012/11 /republicans-gerrymandering-house-representatives-election-chart.

17. Ibid.

18. Ibid.

19. Tom Perkins, "Once again, Michigan Dems receive more votes in the State House, but Republicans hold onto power," *Detroit Metro Times*, November 16, 2016.

20. Sam Weber and Laura Fong, "North Carolina and Maryland challenge gerrymandering," PBS NewsHour, September 24, 2016.

21. Lauren Harmon and others, "The Health of State Democracies" (Washington: Center for American Progress Action Fund, 2015), available at https://cdn .americanprogressaction.org/wp-content/uploads/2015/07/HSD-report-FINAL.pdf.

22. Thomas E. Mann, "We Must Address Gerrymandering," *Time*, October 13, 2016, available at http://time.com/4527291/2016-election-gerrymandering /?xid=emailshare.

23. John F. Kowal, "When Will Progressives Make Democracy Reform a Top Priority?" Brennan Center for Justice, November 11, 2016, available at https://www .brennancenter.org/blog/when-will-progressives-make-democracy-reform-top-priority.

24. Shawn Johnson, "Democrats Ask Court to Consider 2016 Results In Gerrymander Disputes," Wisconsin Public Radio, November 16, 2016.

25. Dan Vicuña, Keshia Morris, and Dale Eisman, "Restoring Voter Choice: How Citizen-Led Redistricting Can End the Manipulation of Our Elections" (Washington: Common Cause, 2016), available at http://www.restoringvoterchoice.org/.

26. Ibid.

27. Dan Vicuña, "Gerrymander Gazette," Common Cause, November 23, 2016.

28. Ibid.

29. Harmon and others, "The Health of State Democracies."

30. Ibid.

31. Ballotpedia, "State-by-state redistricting procedures," available at https://ballotpedia .org/State-by-state_redistricting_procedures (last accessed November 2016).

32. Vicuña, Morris, and Eisman, "Restoring Voter Choice."

33. Katie J.M. Baker, "Michigan Likely to Pass Abortion Bill Democrats Dub 'Rape Insurance,'" *Newsweek*, December 4, 2013, available at http://www.newsweek.com /latest-challenge-womens-right-abortion-defies-majority-michigan-216774.

34. Public Policy Polling, "Michiganders Support More LGBT Protections," July 1, 2015, available at http://www.publicpolicypolling.com/main/2015/07/michiganders -support-more-lgbt-protections.html.

35. Mark Joseph Stern, "Michigan Legislature Passes Bills Allowing Adoption Agencies to Turn Away Gay Couples," Slate, June 5, 2015, available at http://www.slate.com /blogs/outward/2015/06/10/michigan_legislature_passes_anti_gay_adoption_bills .html.

36. Paul Egan, "Is emergency manager law to blame for Flint water crisis?" *Detroit Free Press*, October 25, 2015, available at http://www.freep.com/story/news /politics/2015/10/24/emergency-manager-law-blame-flint-water-crisis/74048854/.

37. Ibid.; Claire Groden, "Emergency Manager System Comes Under Fire After Flint Water Disaster," *Fortune*, March 23, 2016, available at http://fortune.com/2016/03/23 /flint-emergency-managers/.

38. Ballotpedia, "State-by-state redistricting procedures," available at https://ballotpedia .org/State-by-state_redistricting_procedures (last accessed November 2016).

39. Vicuña, Morris, and Eisman, "Restoring Voter Choice."

40. Intelligence Squared Debates, "Gerrymandering Is Destroying the Political Center," November 14, 2016, available at http://www.intelligencesquaredus.org/debates /gerrymandering-destroying-political-center.

41. Idaho Const. art. III, § 2.

42. Mo. Const. art. III, §§ 2, 7; Levitt, "A Citizens Guide to Redistricting."

43. N.J. Const. art. IV, § 3, ¶ 2 (requiring the Chief Justice of the Supreme Court to appoint a tiebreaker).

44. Levitt, "A Citizens Guide to Redistricting."

45. Justin Levitt, "California," All About Redistricting, available at http://redistricting.lls .edu/states-CA.php (last accessed November 2016).

46. Ibid.

47. Ibid.

48. Ibid.

49. Ibid.

50. Ibid.

51. Ibid.

52. Common Cause, "California Voters Pass Sweeping Democracy Reform"; Aleah Jennings-Newhouse, Sydney Fix, and Malini Ramaiyer, "City measures T1, U1, V1, W1, X1, Y1, Z1, AA pass; measures BB, CC, DD fail," *The Daily Californian*, November 9, 2016, available at http://www.dailycal.org/2016/11/09/city-measures -t1-u1-v1-w1-x1-y1-z1-aa-pass-measures-bb-cc-dd-fail/.

53. *The Sacramento Bee*, "Fix Sacramento's local election map with Measure L," September 8, 2016, available at http://www.sacbee.com/opinion/election -endorsements/article100705902.html.

54. Ibid.

55. Alexandra Yoon-Hendricks and Andrea Platten, "12 Berkeley Ballot Measures for November 2016 Election," *The Daily Californian*, October 28, 2016, available at http://www.dailycal.org/2016/10/28/12-berkeley-ballot-measures-for-november -2016-election/.

56. Ibid.

57. Ibid.

58. Arizona Independent Redistricting Commission, "Mission," available at http:// azredistricting.org/ (last accessed November 2016).

59. *Arizona State Legislature v. Arizona Independent Redistricting Commission*, 576 U.S. ____ (2015), available at https://www.supremecourt.gov/opinions/14pdf/13-1314_ kjfl.pdf.

60. Ibid.

61. Ibid.

62. Justin Levitt, "Where are the lines drawn? – congressional districts," All About Redistricting, available at http://redistricting.lls.edu/where-tablefed.php (last accessed November 2016).

63. Ibid.

64. Ibid.

65. Fla. Const., Amdt. 5. See also, Brennan Center for Justice, "Florida: Status Quo," available at https://www.brennancenter.org/sites/default/files/analysis/FL.pdf (last accessed December 2016).

66. *League of Women Voters of Florida v. Detzner*, 173 So.3d 963 (Fla. 2014).

67. Ibid.

68. Cal. Const. art. XXI, § 2(h).

69. Levitt, "A Citizens Guide to Redistricting."

2

Math Equations Could Help Fight Gerrymandering

Matt Pancia

People's Policy Project is a think tank that publishes ideas and analysis that assist in the development of an economic system that serves the many, not the few.

On Election Day in 2010, Republicans flipped nineteen legislative seats and took control of ten states. However, this victory wasn't a surprise. The outcome of the election had been the product of years of work by the Republican Party. It was called REDMAP (REDistricting Majority Project), and its single goal was to specifically win elections that would enable the Republican Party to control the next round of redistricting. As viewpoint author Matt Pancia shows, REDMAP continues to win elections. Gerrymandering is poorly defined legally, making it hard to fight, but the use of a mathematical equation known as "the efficiency gap" could help define gerrymandering in a more objective way.

In the 2012 Pennsylvania statehouse elections, 51% of the vote went to Democrats, but they received only 28% of the representatives. This wasn't a fluke—in 6 other states Democrats received a *minority* fraction of state representatives while obtaining a *majority* of the votes, a pattern mirrored in federal elections. These results, declared a "shellacking" by President Obama, gave us

"The Problem of Defining Gerrymandering," by Matt Pancia, People's Policy Project, October 17, 2017. Reprinted by permission.

a Republican majority in the House, created an entrenched Freedom Caucus, and produced several other equally-grim side-effects.

The origins of this strange mathematical phenomenon appear two years prior, in a gust of what is now seen to have been some incredibly effective political spending. Under the banner of REDMAP, Republicans pumped the relatively small sum of $30 million into targeted local races, taking control of several state legislatures. This granted them the power to redraw some congressional and state district maps after the census, which they quickly took advantage of.

Seeking district maps that benefitted them, mapmakers employed tactics like "packing" Democrats into small numbers of districts or "cracking" dense populations of Democrats (usually in cities) into multiple, sprawling districts where their votes were diluted by rural Republican voters. Access to unprecedented amounts of voter data and powerful predictive algorithms made this easy, and resulted in maps that served their makers extremely well.

Drawing congressional districts that end up favoring a *political party or candidate* is called *partisan gerrymandering*, and is, in fact, illegal. How was this allowed to happen, then, with Republican operatives like Karl Rove brazenly declaring, "He who controls redistricting can control Congress"?

Legal Background and Current Case

The answer comes from the Supreme Court. Over 30 years ago in *Davis v. Bandemer*, they declared "extreme" partisan gerrymandering unconstitutional, but failed to establish a standard for use in determining if it was happening at all. Lower courts have searched for such a standard ever since, but the Supreme Court has yet to accept any of them.

The plaintiffs in the current Supreme Court case, *Gill v. Whitford*, hope to change this. If the court rules in their favor, lower courts will be freed from their current paralysis, allowing for successful legal challenges to gerrymandered maps.

Gill reviews a decision to invalidate the Wisconsin state legislature map for illegally favoring Republicans, who won around

60% of the state assembly seats with only 49% of the votes in 2012. The skew seems obvious, so why is there any controversy around this case?

While the outcome of the election feels very wrong, proportional party representation is not a *legal* requirement for district maps. The law requires instead that plaintiffs show an *asymmetrical, persistent* bias against a particular political party. A lack of an agreed-upon method for showing this has been the biggest barrier in establishing a gerrymandering standard.

This is why the *Gill* plaintiffs engaged in a more complicated analysis in their claim. They rely on a computed quantity (or "metric") called the "Efficiency Gap" (EG), meant to measure the number of "wasted votes" cast for a given political party.

Their argument is based on the idea that the EG of the current map against the Democrats is unreasonably, persistently large and as a result, the votes of Democrats in Wisconsin were disproportionately wasted.

If the court rejects this argument, the Wisconsin map will stand. There will continue to be no legal apparatus to challenge current gerrymanders or to prevent more egregious ones being drawn after the 2020 census—and, to be clear, they *will* be more egregious.

Republicans are already teeing up REDMAP 2020, expecting to spend at least $125 million to push for further gerrymandering. The Democrats plan to launch their own PAC to counter the Republicans, an effort that could easily fail. The likely outcome of this will be, in the words of the *Gill* plaintiffs, "a festival of copycat gerrymandering the likes of which this country has never seen."

What If SCOTUS Rules Against Wisconsin?

Even if such an apocalyptic scenario is averted by an invalidation of the Wisconsin map, partisan gerrymandering isn't necessarily dead.

Court Cases Could Be Lost

A decision for the plaintiffs would simply leave room for gerrymandering cases to be decided in court, which could result in several problems, the first being that these cases will be *messy.*

In court, those that defend gerrymandered maps will have the opportunity to intentionally misrepresent or misunderstand the arguments presented to show that gerrymandering has occurred. In addition, the technical nature of these arguments means that there might be confusion in the debate around them, undermining the ability of well-meaning judges to arrive at correct conclusions. The history of racial gerrymandering cases tells us that this is a dangerous possibility and, moreover, both have already happened in *Gill.*

If this happens with a relatively simple metric like the EG, it is bound to happen with more sophisticated tests that will arise in the future, and doesn't bode well for our ability to quickly strike down gerrymandered maps.

Unintended Consequences

Even if these court battles work out in our collective favor, congressional maps must still be drawn, and the legal standards set in gerrymandering cases could influence this process.

By latching on too hard to metrics like the EG in calling out gerrymandering, minimizing them might be taken as a *goal*, and in doing so we risk incorporating the political biases of those metrics into new maps.

Some of the biases of the EG are revealed with simple algebra, indicating that its use can:

- discourage proportional party allocation of representatives;
- encourage uncompetitive districts;
- be unpredictable in competitive races;
- fail to allow for any maps that aren't considered gerrymandered;
- force drawing of bizarrely shaped districts.

It could get worse: the use of more sophisticated computational techniques and statistical methods will introduce biases that their users may not know of. Recent usages of machine learning techniques provide awful examples, and there is not a known way of avoiding this.

As a result, we could end up accidentally drawing maps with completely undesirable, unpredicted political properties.

An Arms Race

The final problem is technological: our tools to fight gerrymandering might not be good enough.

Much like online spammers trying to outsmart email filters, perpetrators of gerrymandering will constantly engage in developing more advanced ways to undermine *any* court-established gerrymandering tests.

With relative ease, a mapmaker can tell a computer, "Draw a legally acceptable map that maximizes the number of seats that the Republicans are going to pick up while still having an EG less than 7%."

Electoral polarization and the mountains of micro-targeted demographic and political data available to data scientists may make this a feasible problem to solve, producing gerrymandered maps that, from the perspective of the courts, don't look it.

Because intent is not enough to invalidate a map, this is completely legal. Maps can be implemented that were constructed with the explicit goal of fooling whatever test is being used at the moment—provided that they have succeeded in doing so. Those on the other side will be forced to improve their own anti-gerrymandering techniques to keep up in court, and they might not succeed.

Jordan Ellenberg, a mathematician involved in gerrymandering research, describes the arms race this sets up succinctly:

> You can use [advanced computation] to make electoral mischief, but you can also use it to detect and measure that mischief. It's not math versus democracy; it's math versus math, with democracy at stake.

On one side of this battle are academics, lawyers and others working to develop better methods for defining and detecting gerrymandering. On the other side are political operatives with vast private data and cynical political motivations.

One of these sides has access to far more resources than the other, and it's not the one that we'd want to win.

Conclusion

All of the above suggests that contending with the existence of gerrymandered maps will be difficult. We'd be better off stopping them from being drawn in the first place.

Luckily, there are a variety of popular, relatively mild political options to do so at our disposal, the most effective of which would be requiring transparent, independent commissions to draw district maps.

If done correctly, this would eliminate the structural problem of legislators being in a position of power to draw the district maps that they stand to benefit from. Six states already have already done so, and the resulting maps seem to produce more competitive congressional races.

There are also more radical, better alternatives worth considering. Changing the voting system to one that provides proportional representation would end gerrymandering, and some proposals eliminate district maps entirely, getting rid of racial gerrymandering, partisan gerrymandering, and potential bias in one fell swoop.

No matter what, it's imperative that we implement *some* reforms to curb gerrymandering—if we don't, we'll be permanently left with rigged maps, an unresponsive legislature, and a thoroughly broken democracy.

3

Aims and Tactics of Modern Gerrymandering

Greg Gillette

United States Common Sense is a nonprofit policy group founded at Stanford University. It is dedicated to educating the public on how the government functions.

There are two main types of gerrymandering that occur in the United States, racial and partisan. While the Supreme Court has made it clear that racial gerrymandering that's done to silence minority voters is illegal, its rules for partisan gerrymandering are less clear. As Greg Gillette points out, while many legal cases about partisan gerrymandering have made it to the Supreme Court, so far they have not set clear guidelines for the legality of partisan gerrymandering. In the absence of clear legal standards, it is up to the states to defend voters against gerrymandering. Gillette outlines successful steps some states have taken to prevent gerrymandering.

In Brief

Gerrymandering refers to the intentional manipulation of district boundaries to create predictable, "safe districts" for political gain. A component of US politics since as early as 1788, gerrymandering is widely considered a negative element of the political system as it creates political advantage for incumbent representatives and parties by limiting election competitiveness. This brief describes gerrymandering and its different forms, and reviews states' efforts to combat it.

"What Is Gerrymandering?" by Greg Gillette, United States Common Sense, December 9, 2015. Reprinted by permission.

Overview: District Boundaries, Equal Representation, and Gerrymandering

Elected representatives in the US House of Representatives, state legislatures, and most municipalities represent voters within a specified district boundary. For voters to have equal legislative representation through their elected representatives, districts must have approximately equally sized populations. This concept is commonly summarized as the US Supreme Court's "one person, one vote" standard articulated in a series of rulings in the 1960s.

However, district populations grow and shrink unevenly over time, meaning, periodically (once per decade), district boundaries must be redrawn, or redistricted, to restore roughly equal legislative representation. In 37 states, elected state legislators have control over redistricting, including the areas they each represent. They can determine the populations that constitute their districts, using various tactics to include populations most likely to support them in re-election and excluding those least likely to support them. When legislators design voting boundaries to meet their political aims rather than to restore equal representation, it is known as gerrymandering.

Gerrymandering Aims and Tactics

Gerrymandering refers to any deliberate manipulation of electoral district borders. Two common types of gerrymandering in modern US politics are racial and partisan gerrymandering.

Racial gerrymandering occurs when legislators draw districts to reduce the impact of racial minority voters. This violates the Voting Rights Act of 1965 and the Supreme Court has consistently declared specific instances unconstitutional. However, it is legal for legislators to enhance racial minorities' collective voting influence by concentrating minority voters within a voting district, which is called affirmative racial gerrymandering.

Partisan gerrymandering aims to minimize the impact of opposition voters for a specific candidate or issue. Legislators may "crack" up opposition voters so their votes will have less impact on any one district. Legislators may also "pack" one district with opposition voters so their votes play a less significant role in remaining districts. These tactics often lead to the odd shapes associated with gerrymandered districts as niche, but often geographically dispersed, areas need to be connected.

The Supreme Court has heard many cases regarding partisan gerrymandering but has never established a clear standard for adjudicating partisan gerrymandering claims. Without such a standard, no case has been overturned and partisan gerrymandering remains a common, legal practice.

How Do States Combat Gerrymandering?

Analysts attribute gerrymandering to the control incumbent elected officials have over the redistricting process. Currently, 37 state legislatures have control over drawing their own districts and 42 state legislatures have control over drawing House districts. In an effort to limit gerrymandering, some states have reduced legislative control by establishing separate commissions to advise or control the redistricting process:

- Advisory commissions consist of non-legislators, usually appointed by legislators. The commission provides input, but legislators retain redistricting power and are not bound by the input.
- Backup commissions are also appointed by legislators, and are asked to provide input if legislatures cannot pass a plan by a specified deadline.
- Politician commissions consist of non-elected officials.
- Independent commissions are comprised of non-legislators and non-public officials who are often prohibited from running for public office within a specific period of time after they serve on the independent redistricting commission. Independent commissions are generally considered the gold standard against gerrymandering.

Summary

- Gerrymandering is the intentional manipulation of district boundaries to concentrate specific voting populations for political gain.
- "Cracking" and "packing" are common gerrymandering tactics used to dilute the representation of likely oppositional voters.
- Typically, state legislators are responsible for re-drawing district boundaries and do so to benefit their party's or their own political outcomes.
- The US Supreme Court has not heard partisan gerrymandering cases, and the practice is both common and legal.
- Some states have removed elected officials from the redistricting process to prevent gerrymandering.

4

Single-Member Elections Lead to Less Democratic and Representative Elections

Kristin Eberhard

Kristin Eberhard is a senior researcher and political policy enthusiast. She researches, writes, and speaks about climate change policy and democracy reform.

Voters have power when politicians need their votes to win. When politicians can gerrymander districts, it means they no longer need to consider the opinion of those unlikely to vote for them. Kristin Eberhard describes how politicians use tactics known as "cracking" and "packing" to create districts where only their supporters' votes matter. When only one demographic's votes matter, it creates "wasted votes," something researchers call the "efficiency gap." She argues that while there are many techniques that could be used to test for and solve the efficiency gap, allowing voters to elect more than one person per election would ultimately lead to fairer elections overall.

When you take the trouble to vote, you want it to matter that you did. You want your vote to make a difference in who gets elected. You want your vote to elect someone you like, so that for the next few years you can know that person is in office, shaping policy on issues that are important to you.

"Slaying the Gerrymander, Part 2: Make More Votes Matter," by Kristin Eberhard, Sightline Institute, August 3, 2017. Reprinted by permission.

But single-winner districts and the gerrymander sap voters' power by wasting their votes in two ways: predetermining winners in safe districts and denying many voters the power to elect a representative. If your district is safe for one party or the other, it won't much matter whether you vote—if you hold the minority view, you'll never be able to elect a like-minded representative, and if you hold the majority view, your candidate will win in a landslide so it won't matter if you stay home. About half the votes in safe districts won't matter. If your district is competitive then it will matter that you turn out to vote, but there is about a 50 percent chance you'll end up with no one representing your views in the legislature. About half the voters in each competitive district will be unrepresented.

If you are an American or Canadian who has never known anything but this wasteful electoral system, the math might seem inevitable to you. You might be shrugging, thinking: "Some voters vote for the loser. That's just life." You might be thinking of elections like a football or hockey game: "One team wins, the other loses. So yeah, half the teams lose, so what? *Everyone* doesn't get a trophy!"

Electing a president might be like a football game, with just one winner and lots of disappointed fans of the losing team. But electing a legislature is more like ordering a bunch of pitchers of beer for a group of people watching the football game. Since there are lots of pitchers, almost everyone at the table should be able to drink something they like. If half or more of the people at the table asked for the beer they liked but didn't get it, they wouldn't just shrug and say "I voted for the losing beer. That's just life." They would demand a say in choosing at least one of the pitchers. Similarly, if there are lots of legislators, every voter should have a say in electing at least one representative they like.

Unfortunately, no amount of tweaking the gerrymander in single-winner districts will ensure that your vote matters and that you can elect someone you like. But multi-member districts let voters choose multiple pitchers of beer, so to speak.

Wasted Votes Are a Mathematical Certainty in Single-Member Districts

A powerful vote is one that a candidate *needs* to get elected and that *succeeds* in electing that candidate. A wasted vote is one that is *unnecessary (surplus)* because the candidate would have won anyway, or *unsuccessful (lost)* because the candidate does not win. To American or Canadian voters this probably sounds like just the way things work—sometimes your candidate wins by a lot and sometimes she doesn't win, but that doesn't mean your vote was wasted, it just means that's how the election turned out. But surplus and lost votes are the gerrymander's weapons. The heart of the gerrymandering case going before the US Supreme Court is a test that measures how many votes for each party were wasted (surplus or lost).

Intentional partisan gerrymandering uses two strategies to waste the other party's votes. First, line-drawers can "pack" one party's voters into safe districts where the winner has a huge surplus beyond what they need to win. Before any candidate has declared his candidacy, long before voters fill in their ballots, the race can already be called just by looking at the district lines. By herding one party's voters into this one district, line-drawers create many surplus votes for that party and deny those additional voters the ability to elect an additional representative.

Second, the line-drawers can "crack" voters across competitive districts where many of their votes are lost on a losing candidate. In competitive districts nearly half of voters vote for the loser, meaning their vote didn't have the power to elect a representative. By drawing lines that barely tip the advantage to their own party, line-drawers ensure that the other party wastes close to half the votes in that district.

If a party can draw district after district where the other party is either winning in a landslide (wasting surplus votes) or just barely losing (wasting nearly half its votes), it can circumvent the will of the people, ensuring the line-drawers' party gets more seats than it has votes. For example, in the gerrymandering case the US

Supreme Court will hear this fall, Wisconsin's Republican-drawn district maps enabled Republicans to win more than 60 percent of seats in the state house despite winning less than 49 percent of the vote.

No, That Big Supreme Court Gerrymandering Case Won't Ensure Your Vote Matters

The US Supreme Court has previously declined to strike down partisan gerrymandering because it didn't have a reliable test for identifying partisan gerrymandering. But it recently agreed to hear a partisan gerrymandering case, signalling that it might be ready to adopt the test the appeals court used. The federal court of appeals used a three-pronged test to determine that the district maps were illegally gerrymandered:

1. the district line-drawers *intended* to disempower voters of one political party,
2. the district maps had that effect, and
3. the maps could not be justified on other grounds.

To prove the second prong—that the maps disproportionately wasted one party's votes—the court used the "efficiency gap," a formula researchers developed for measuring how many votes for each party were wasted.

But even if the court uses the analysis of wasted votes to strike down extreme partisan gerrymandering, no one can change the fact that in every single-winner district, half the votes are surplus or lost. If a redistricting map passes the "efficiency gap" test, it just means that roughly half of *both* Democratic *and* Republican votes are wasted.

Other academics have proposed alternative ways for the court to test whether district maps unfairly waste more votes from one party than the other, including geometric compactness scores, computational methods, computer programs, and a mathematical index. All of these tests could improve the fairness between the two major parties, but none can protect you, the voter, and ensure your vote matters. Ironically, as explained in Part 1 of this series, more competitive districts might lead to fewer voters having a like-minded representative. If every district contains about half Democrats and half Republicans, then half the voters won't have a representative they like. If you are a voter in a competitive district, there is about a 50 percent chance you'll end up with no one representing your views in the legislature.

With Multi-Member Districts, Your Vote Matters and You Can Elect a Representative You Like

Americans and Canadians are so accustomed to anachronistic single-member districts, we might not even realize we should be outraged at our lack of power and lack of representation. We reason that, when electing a president or a governor or a mayor, only one person wins—there's just one trophy. Mathematically, many opposition voters will inevitably be unhappy with the outcome. And we accept the same level of unhappiness with legislatures.

But legislatures are different. There are many legislators. Many people get a trophy, so to speak. The whole point of electing 435 United States representatives or 98 Washington representatives or 60 Oregon representatives is that there are lots of them and they can represent a diversity of voters. There's no reason for half or more of voters to settle for *no representation* in a multi-member body like a legislature.

Most developed democracies figured this out during the twentieth century and adopted electoral methods that gave more voters more power to elect legislators of their choice. Different countries accomplish this in different ways, but they all have one thing in common: they don't use single-member districts. They let voters have a say in electing a group of legislators at once. One way that Americans and Canadians could finally get around to doing this would be to use multi-member districts and let voters rank their choices.

For example, in Washington state, voters already elect three representatives (one state senator and two state representatives) from a district. But they vote for each one separately. Imagine instead you elected them all at once. Same number of options on the ballot, same number of representatives for the district. Instead of seeing six candidates listed two at a time in three different races electing a total of three people, you would see six candidates listed in one race electing a total of three people. You rank your choices. Say your first-choice candidate, Felicia Fund College, loses. The way we vote now, your vote would effectively be thrown in the trash and you'd tell yourself "I voted for the loser. That's life."

With a ranked ballot, your vote would get transferred to your next-ranked candidate still in the running. Say your next choice was Maria Moderate. But she is quite popular and already has 10 percent more votes than she needs to win a seat. Instead of those extra votes being surplus (wasted), all of Maria's voters have 90 percent of their vote contribute to her win, and 10 percent of their vote transferred to their next-ranked candidate who is still in the running. Everyone's entire vote has the chance to elect candidates they like; none of it is wasted. Every voter gets exactly one vote, but every vote counts towards electing one or more of the three representatives.

Don't Settle

Americans and Canadians are so used to wasting our votes in legislative elections, we have come to think of it as inevitable. But wasted votes, and gerrymandering the lines to waste more of some people's votes than others, are only inevitable if we choose to use single-member districts. Multi-member districts deal a death blow to the gerrymander by making most votes matter.

5

A Brief History of Gerrymandering Legal Cases

Matthew Spector

Matthew Spector is a master's in public policy candidate at the John F. Kennedy School of Government and is a former visiting researcher in governance studies at the Brookings Institution.

In this viewpoint, Matthew Spector of the Brookings Institution summarizes the history of gerrymandering lawsuits. He begins with Davis v. Bandemer, *which noted that partisan gerrymandering was unconstitutional but set standards that made it difficult to prove. Challengers not only had to prove that maps were drawn with the intent to discriminate against a particular demographic, they also had to be able to prove harm was done to that group. The upcoming trial* Gill v. Whitford *offers the Supreme Court another chance to define a firm and testable legal standard for measuring gerrymandering. This would allow districts all over the United States to challenge redistricting maps.*

Though overshadowed by the first publicly available opinions from Associate Justice Neil Gorsuch, this session of the Supreme Court could prove pivotal for voter representation and the composition of Congress for decades to come.

The Supreme Court's decision to hear *Gill v. Whitford*, in a hearing that will likely take place this fall, will address again

"Supreme Court Set to Scrutinize Partisan Gerrymandering—and Why It Matters," by Matthew Spector, the Brookings Institution, July 19, 2017. Reprinted by permission.

the standards by which partisan redistricting can be challenged. *Gill* matters for the country: states' redistricting following the 2020 Census could welcome new independence—and potentially fix in stone partisan electoral maps for a generation.

Meanwhile, a new bill introduced in the House by Democrats last month, though unlikely to pass, attempts to circumvent partisanship in redistricting altogether with a new model. Both have struck a nerve: *Gill* in particular ignites fresh debate as to the nature of equal representation in coming electoral cycles.

A Mixed Judicial History on Gerrymandering

The court's track record has been mixed, and thus far relatively unclear, on the standards to which it can rule in assessing states' political gerrymandering.

The court ruled in 1986's *Davis v. Bandemer* that although partisan gerrymandering was addressable by the court under the Fourteenth Amendment's "equal protection clause" and under the First Amendment's right to political expression, it limited the bases upon which entities could challenge district apportionment.

Gerrymandering was indeed unconstitutional, but a degree of harm needed to be proven. Reversing the district court's decision, the court asserted redistricting could be deemed unconstitutional if claimants had proven "both intentional discrimination against an identifiable political group and an actual discriminatory effect on that group." This distinction of "intentional" and "actual" discrimination would prove hard to validate—claimants would need to prove successive elections failed to allow "one person, one vote" *with intent*. One justice even challenged whether the Supreme Court and other federal courts should be able to address these political questions altogether.

The standard for partisan gerrymandering remained difficult to define. In 2003, a conservative-leaning court in *Vieth v. Jubelirer* claimed the court could not decide on these matters, citing "no judicially discernible and manageable standards for adjudicating such claims exist." It invalidated the *Davis* standard, and without a hard measure of what partisanship and fair political representation could entail, it further muddled and limited the role of the court in these matters.

Why *Gill* Matters

The *Cooper v. Harris* decision this year deemed certain North Carolina redistricting plans unconstitutional on the grounds of racial gerrymandering. Now the court's upcoming *Gill v. Whitford* hearing might establish new a standard for partisan gerrymandering.

In *Gill*, Wisconsin appealed a federal court's 2016 decision invalidating the state's post-2010 redistricting map. In the first federal ruling striking down a map for partisan gerrymandering in more than 30 years, the panel deemed Wisconsin's Republican-led legislature's 2011 map as unconstitutional on First and Fourteenth Amendment bases.

In arguing *Gill* in the Supreme Court, the plaintiffs' novel approach might answer the question of partisan "standards" once and for all. The nonprofit Campaign Legal Center (CLC) has challenged Wisconsin's redistricting map by applying a numerical standard, testing the applicability of a mathematical device called the "efficiency gap," developed by two University of Chicago scholars. The efficiency gap applies a measure of "wasted votes"—votes wasted if cast for a losing candidate or a winning candidate beyond those needed to win the election. Across the nearly thirty years of voting measurement, the scholars' analysis found "the severity of today's gerrymandering is…unprecedented in modern times."

Higher courts have thus far affirmed the challenges to Wisconsin's map. If the Supreme Court rules for the "efficiency gap" proponents, it will have finally set a hard and testable legal standard in "wasted votes" against which future apportionments might be challenged.

Given the degree of population shifts in rust belt states, the 2020 census could stand to redefine districts and, more critically, the electoral map and parties' calculus. If the courts define a standard for these challenges, partisan groups across the political spectrum could challenge redistricting maps, leading to a flood of legal activity using that new standard. If the courts rule there is no reasonable standard for challenge, there may be no possible route for future challenges, cementing redistricting maps as legislatures define them.

Combating Fatalistic Voter Behavior

Alongside new legal challenges that have raised awareness of gerrymandering, some members of Congress have identified an opening for a new approach.

In June, Rep. Don Beyer (D-Va.)—a longtime proponent of independent redistricting—introduced the Fair Representation Act alongside Democratic colleagues. The Act proposes a shift to larger multimember, "proportionally representative" districts for states with six or more representatives and recommends funding for a new model for rank ordering.

The current "winner-take-all" model creates Congressional districts that advocates like Third Way and FairVote claim has created deeper ideological division and served to systematically sow voter underrepresentation, often and likely in violation of Section 2 of the Voting Rights Act. The zero-sum system has produced electoral outcomes like that of 2012, where Democrats in aggregate received roughly 1.5 million more votes than Republicans, yet Republicans retained a more than 30-seat majority in the House—an outcome advocates claimed was the result of "packing and wasting" of votes through gerrymandering.

In Western Europe, rank ordering has been proven a "more accurate" voting system for races with more than two candidates. In focusing on district magnitude and ballot structure, proponents argue rank ordering would negate additional complex, and costly, runoff elections—and more critically help promote electoral processes that are "less negative," more civil and more likely to foster compromise.

For equitable vote advocates, the lack of middle ground has exposed how unsustainable winner-take-all has become, and made clear the need for fundamental change. States like Massachusetts are only represented by Democrats in Congress, while several Midwest states only send Republicans to the House. Both fail to represent their significant voter identification with both parties, leading to reduced trust among the represented. Beyer and his colleagues believe a "fairer" voting process can rebuild this common ground.

That Democrats are the sole sponsors of this bill underscores how fundamental legislation of this kind would most likely never pass the House, let alone the Senate, given the current political economy of voting rights. Republicans' well-publicized REDMAP project strategy, the "packing and cracking" districts to drive a blue-to-red shift larger "than either party has seen in modern history," has succeeded. The strategy, largely executed through partisan control of state legislatures, continues to bear fruit despite the challenges described above. This status quo means incumbents are now more concerned about challenges from primary opponents than from their opposing party.

Even independent redistricting bodies like the State of Arizona's commission, once established, fall prey to partisan infighting, and require court intervention to determine whether state legislatures could be removed from redistricting altogether (they could). Any successes in implementing independent or non-partisan redistricting would likely benefit Democrats; that discomfort, and increasing polarization, make consensus and independent "balanced" districts far less likely.

Bottom Line

As the weight and consequence of voting behavior becomes more salient for voters and communities, the coming year might represent a turning point for equal representation. Given the new standard of partisanship it tests, *Gill v Whitford* is a vital case for parties and state legislators to observe; while political ideologies appear more fixed than ever, district maps are anything but.

6

Elections in the US Could Be Improved, But No Electoral System Is Perfect

Kristin Eberhard

Kristin Eberhard is a senior researcher and political policy enthusiast. She researches, writes, and speaks about climate change policy and democracy reform.

The United States isn't the only democratic nation to suffer from gerrymandering. Cascadia is the popular name for a region of North America that encompasses Oregon; Washington; British Columbia, Canada; and some neighboring regions. This viewpoint discusses how gerrymandering affects both American and Canadian citizens of the Cascadia region. Kristin Eberhard describes alternative districting and electoral procedures that could lead to fairer, more representative elections. Unfortunately, there are few systems that cannot be abused in some manner, so Eberhard also points out the problems that could arise from each of these systems. One thing that remains clear: elections across North America could be more democratic.

The legislature is the people's house, the hall of a representative democracy where representatives of the people meet to craft solutions to pressing problems. It is the body that takes people's values and puts them into action. That's the ideal. And when it works well, it's golden.

"Sightline's Guide to Methods for Electing Legislative Bodies," by Kristin Eberhard, Sightline Institute, May 18, 2017. Reprinted by permission.

For example, the US Congress turned people's growing concern about labor conditions during the Progressive Era into child labor and minimum wage laws; the Oregon state legislature's leadership on the bottle bill enacted community values about protecting the environment; Washington's state legislature responded to changing public sentiment by legalizing marriage equality; and British Columbia acted on people's concerns about climate change by enacting a tax on carbon pollution.

But it doesn't always work that way. In fact, in the United States and Canada, federal, state, and provincial legislatures often don't reflect or act on the views and values of the people. They become mired in gridlock and political grandstanding, seeking quick fixes and catering to special interests. The media talk more about representatives' hairstyles, emails, and personal lives than community challenges and solutions, leaving voters ill-informed about policy they could urge their representatives to enact.

What other options do Cascadians have for electing more reflective and effective legislative bodies? This article gives Sightline's take on what is important in a method for electing a legislative body, including city and county councils, and how different election methods could achieve results that get closer—more often and more deeply—to the ideal where electeds work for the people who put them in office, rather than for special interests or narrow or extreme slices of the electorate. The theme throughout is: homogenous legislatures including only, say, white men with a narrow range of political ideologies or life experiences, produce poor results for a diverse electorate, while diverse legislatures, including people with many different life experiences and political perspectives, produce better results.

Election methods aren't the only factor. Big money in politics and barriers to voting can prevent people from having a say in who gets elected, and structural barriers in the candidate pipeline can block diverse candidates. Elections are not a silver bullet, but improving how we vote could be a hefty piece of silver buckshot in the quest to make democracy in Cascadia and throughout the United States and Canada more representative.

Our Glossary of Methods for Electing Legislative Bodies describes nine different ways to elect a legislature, categorized into four families:

- In Majoritarian methods, used in the United States and Canada, all or most legislators represent majority views, while minority groups do not have fair representation. Usually, two major parties representing the social or political majority dominate the legislature.
- In Proportional methods, used in most developed countries, legislators represent the diversity of voters. Usually, several parties representing a range of social and political views win seats in proportion to the votes they receive.
- In Semi-proportional methods, used in local elections across the United States, minority social or political groups have a chance to win seats.
- Potentially Proportional methods have not been used in any public elections, but might achieve proportional results.

Research reveals stark differences between majoritarian and proportional methods. For each of the properties we identified below as being broken about the political systems in the United States and Canada, proportional election methods offer a solution.

Semi-proportional methods are used at the local but not the national level anywhere in the world, so there is much less research on their outcomes, and the sections below only discuss majoritarian and proportional methods. The effects of semi-proportional methods tend to fall somewhere in the middle, depending on the specific circumstances in which they are implemented.

Two Potentially Proportional methods have not yet been used in any public elections but theoretically could achieve proportional results. They would likely achieve many of the benefits that semi-proportional methods yield, and possibly more.

Majoritarian Methods Have Problems; Proportional Methods Have Solutions

The United States and Canada primarily use majoritarian election methods—particularly single-winner, "vote for one" elections—to elect federal, state, and provincial legislatures, local councils, and school boards. These methods lead to many problems. But decades of research on countries using different election methods show a better way forward with proportional methods. Proportional electoral methods elect more representative legislatures, defang gerrymandering, empower voters, lead to long-term policy solutions, and counter the power of extractive special interests.

The Best Election Reform Options for Cascadia

Clearly, proportional election methods win. But *which* proportional method should reformers in Cascadia push for? Sightline's view is that advocates should prioritize the election methods that work best *and* are most likely be used in other cities, counties, states, and provinces across Cascadia, in order to make sure that the effort required to win each reform builds momentum for future wins. In other words, the best systems in Cascadia are those that provide diverse representation, can do so at multiple levels of government so that Cascadian cities, counties, state and provinces can try them out, and preferably, have a track record that can help voters be willing to give reform a try.

Multi-winner Ranked-Choice Voting, a.k.a. Single Transferable Vote, can be used in local or nonpartisan elections, which could help introduce Cascadian voters to the concept and build momentum for reform up the chain. Multi-winner RCV, which is only currently used in three elections in the United States, requires multi-member districts. Many cities in Oregon and British Columbia already use multi-member districts and Bloc Voting, and could just switch to ranked ballots with no other changes and have proportional representation—voila! But other cities and counties as well as states, provinces, and the federal government would need to change the way they think about districts—and that's an undoubtedly heavy lift. But with that change, cities, counties, states, and provinces in Cascadia could adopt multi-winner RCV and build momentum for sweeping reforms at the national level.

Voters are often reluctant to make big changes to electoral methods, but they may be more willing to adopt reforms that have a track record close to home. For example, Maine voters who adopted Ranked-Choice Voting for state and federal elections may have been reassured that voters in Portland, Maine, had used ranked-choice voting and found it to produce more civil campaigns with broader voter outreach. Here in Cascadia, voters may be interested to hear that Benton County, Oregon, passed a Ranked-Choice Voting initiative in 2016 and even more interested to know how the first election goes in 2018. On the other hand, Cascadian voters who hear that Pierce County tried Instant Runoff Voting and repealed it may be anxious to understand why, and reassured that thirteen US cities and counties already use Ranked-Choice Voting, with proven enhancements to the tone of races and voters' ability to express an opinion about more than one candidate.

Mixed-Member Proportional Voting could be a great solution for federal, state, and provincial elections. Because it retains some single-member districts, it might be an easier transition for American and Canadian voters. Indeed, voters in one Canadian province recently decided to adopt Mixed Member Proportional. New Zealand transitioned from majoritarian to proportional representation by adopting Mixed Member Proportional, with its mix of single-member districts and larger, party-based districts. Because it is party-based, Mixed Member Proportional could not be used in local nonpartisan elections, so it would need to go straight to a win at the state or national level, without testing in local jurisdictions first.

Cascadian cities and counties could use Cumulative Voting in multi-member districts to achieve fairer representation. Cumulative Voting already has a track record in dozens of American jurisdictions, and would involve a relatively simple change to ballots. However, it might not achieve all the benefits of proportional representation described above.

Cities and counties could introduce Reweighted Range Voting or Multi-Winner Score Runoff Voting and potentially achieve proportional representation. However, the pitch to voters would be more challenging since neither these methods, nor any form of score ballot has been used in any public elections anywhere in the world.

Party List Voting is the most proportional of election methods. Because list methods use large districts and party-based voting, they could not be used in local or nonpartisan elections. American voters would likely balk at Closed List Voting, which only allows voters to choose a party and not a candidate. Open List Voting, which allows voters to choose their favorite candidate from party lists, could be more palatable in North America, with its tradition of candidate-focused, rather than party-focused, elections.

Conclusion

Prime Minister Trudeau's 2015 campaign promises of electoral reform indicated Canadians' growing impatience with first-past-the-post voting, and many Americans are also feeling that elections leave much to be desired. Proportional election methods lead to better representation, more voters with more power to elect officials that represent them, less or no risk of gerrymandering, healthy competition among parties presenting policy ideas, and innovative laws that take more voices into account in crafting durable solutions.

Sightline would like to see Cascadian cities, provinces, and states adopt proportional Ranked-Choice Voting or possibly Mixed-Member Proportional Voting for states and provinces. Doing so would improve governance across the region while showing the way for better national methods as well.

Winner-Take-All Elections in Single-Member Districts Are the Root of Gerrymandering

Jais Mehaji

Jais Mehaji is a writer for FairVote, a nonpartisan champion of electoral reforms that give voters greater choice, a stronger voice, and a representative democracy that works for all Americans.

Many think the solution to gerrymandering is to have independent redistricting, meaning politicians would not be allowed to participate in the process of creating districts. This would stop politicians from being able to draw district lines based on where their voters are. However, some think independent redistricting alone cannot solve the problems of gerrymandering. Viewpoint author Jais Mehaji of FairVote advocates for a proportional voting system to create fairer elections. Most US elections are "winner-take-all," which leaves the voices of those who voted for the losing party unheard. By electing more representatives and using proportional voting, voters would have a better chance at being represented by at least one person they choose.

Summary

- Congressional redistricting in Michigan once again has been controversial, with partisan calculations driving many decisions about how district lines were drawn.
- The root of the problem is use of winner-take-all elections in single-member districts in which 51% of voters can elect

"Gerrymandering in Michigan and the Super District Remedy," by Jais Mehaji, Fair Vote, July 20, 2011. Reprinted by permission.

100% of representation. Political activity will have no impact
on representation in a district where one is comfortably
ahead or hopeless behind.

- FairVote has drawn an alternative map based on the most
recent census data that upholds Supreme Court rulings
on equal population while nearly guaranteeing fair
representation for both major parties, a better chance for
independents and competitive voter choice for all Michigan
voters in every election.

Overview

This year's controversies over redistricting in Michigan provide
the latest evidence of the failure of winner-take-all, single member
district rules. Winner-take-all elections inevitably represent many
voters poorly and tempt partisans to gerrymander outcomes. The
1967 law mandating that states use them should be repealed so
that states like Michigan can explore "super district" form of
proportional voting to increase voter choice and fair outcomes.

Used for many national elections and in a growing number
of American cities, proportional voting (sometimes called
"proportional representation") allows like-minded voters to
come together to elect representatives in numbers mirroring
their level of public support—and thereby puts voters in charge
of their representation in every election rather than redistricting
mapmakers once a decade.

The 2011 Congressional Gerrymander

Here's the story from Michigan this year. The state is closely divided
between Republicans and Democrats, but after a near-sweep of the
2010 elections, Republicans have complete control of redistricting.
Last month Republican legislators released their proposed
redistricting plan for the next decade of congressional elections
and have already passed it for Gov. Snyder's expected signature.

As inevitable in a state that does not require independent
redistricting and rewards winner-take-all calculations, the

Republican plan is seen as a partisan gerrymander, although limited by the overall Democratic leanings of the state in federal elections. Democrats hold both of Michigan's US Senate seats and Barack Obama won the state by 16.5% in 2008. Republicans picked up two House seats in 2010 for an overall 9–6 edge and now seek to protect their nine incumbents, with an apparent goal of reducing Democrats to five seats as the state loses a seat due to reapportionment.

In the 2010 plan, Democrats had a partisanship advantage (as measured by whether Barack Obama ran ahead of his national average in the 2008 presidential race) in nine of 15 districts, including five by large margins—not surprising in a state where President Obama ran some 9% ahead of his national average, although limited by the concentrated nature of the Democratic vote in the Detroit area.

In the proposed plan, Democrats would have a partisan advantage in only five seats, with Republicans having an edge in seven seats and two seats evenly balanced. The map represents a risk for Republican in seeking to preserve their nine incumbents. In cutting its advantage closely, no district was drawn where the underlying Republican advantage was greater than 55% to 45% even as four districts have Democratic advantages of at least 60% to 40%. By seeking to keep incumbents safe, it also establishes a winner-take-all ceiling for women challengers in a state where women hold only one US House seat.

Democrats have criticized the plan, but their relative concentration of votes in urban areas makes them vulnerable to such tactics. Democrats and reform watchdogs have criticized the Republican proposal on several grounds:

- *It forces two Democratic incumbents to run against each other, but not Republican incumbents*: Under the new plan, the newly created 9th district will be carved out from a part of the 12th district, which was represented by Rep. Sander Levin (D), and part of the 9th district which was represented by Rep. Gary Peters (D).

- *It seeks to protect all Republican incumbents*: The lines are drawn in a manner designed to protect all nine current Republican incumbents. More Republican territory is added to the first District, for example. Democrats are exploring legal challenges to the Republican plan on constitutional grounds.
- *It "overpacks" African American voters*: Michigan currently has two African American Members of Congress, representing black-majority districts. The new plan keeps these districts as African American majority districts only through devices that make these districts more heavily Democratic and more heavily African American than some observers see as necessary for allowing African Americans to elect candidates of choice in those districts.
- *Contorted geography*: Critics have noted limitations in the compactness and even simple contiguity of the congressional districts. "Defined by isolated islands," districts 9, 10, 11, and 14 are all within a few miles of each other and their shapes are convoluted.
- *Partisan process*: Citing closed meetings, some have suggested the maps were being drawn through a rushed process lacking transparency, having stifled public input and evaded public scrutiny.

A Better Way: Putting Voters in Charge with Proportional Voting

So what should Michigan do? Independent redistricting along the lines of the Iowa model would reduce particularly egregious gerrymandering, but inevitably would still determine representation for most voters, as many districts would end up being noncompetitive due to current concentrations of Republicans and Democrats. It also might continue to "overpack" the Democratic vote in its areas of concentration, leading to statewide outcomes not reflecting statewide voter preference.

To make independent redistricting work, we need to replace winner-take-all elections that disadvantage those in the minority with geographically compact "super districts." In each super district, several representatives would be elected with a proportional voting system like choice voting. Under our proposed plan, Michigan would be divided into four super districts with five seats in Super District 1 (SD1) and three each in SD2, SD3 and SD4. Each district would have the same number of seats per person. (The United States has a long history of multi-seat district elections based on this apportionment principle—e.g., a Maryland House of Delegates district with three seats has three times the number of people as a House of Delegates district with one seat.)

With a proportional voting plan in a three-seat super district, winning a seat would take just over 25% of the vote. Winning two seats would take just over 50% and sweeping all three would take more than 75%. In the five-seat super district, winning one seat would take about 17% of the vote, winning two would take about 34% and winning a majority of three seats would take just over 50%.

Drawing Super Districts for Michigan

To create and evaluate our super districts, we were limited to using districts from the 14 congressional districts as approved by the Republican legislature. We used partisan data about these super districts provided on the Daily Kos blog, using presidential election results from 2008 (We using our variation of the Cook Partisan Voting Index, which was developed in 1997 based on our model that we released earlier that year. We measure the relative performance of the presidential candidates in the district compared to their national average. If Barack Obama ran 5% ahead of his 2008 national average in the super district and John McCain ran 5% below his national average, then the district would have a Democratic partisanship of 55% and a Republican partisanship of 45%.)

Partisan Analysis of Super District Plan

Backers of both major parties would have the power to elect at least one candidate in each our four super districts. Democrats would be favored to earn a 3-2 edge in SD-1, with a chance to earn four seats in a strong Democrat year in which their candidates won two-thirds of the vote in the district. Republicans would be favored to earn a 2-1 edge in SD-4, but would not be guaranteed winning two seats. Absent popular incumbents, the third seat in the remaining districts (SD-2 and SD-3) would also be a toss-up for either party. Minor parties and independents would have a greater chance to win a seat in every district, especially SD-1.

Voting Rights Analysis

We don't have racial data for our proposed plan, but we know that African American voters are relatively concentrated in the Detroit area. African Americans and other racial minorities would not be near the victory threshold in SD-2, SD-3 and SD-4, but their vote still could be influential for influencing who wins In SD-11, African American voters likely are about 25% of the vote, making it easy for those voters to elect one candidate of their choice, and creating a reasonable chance of helping to elect two candidates. Finally, Michigan might well boost its representation of women; today only one of its US House Members is a woman.

Overall, in every district backers of both major parties would almost certainly end up with a representative of their preferred party and have a reason to vote in a competitive election every two years. Using this proportional voting system would ensure Michigan's electoral outcomes reflect the reality that Democrats have a slight advantage in the state overall, but Republicans can make the state highly competitive. It would mitigate the pernicious effects of gerrymandering that plague our democracy.

8

The Supreme Court Must Decide the Legality of Using Computer Algorithms to Draw Districts

Nina Totenberg

Nina Totenberg is NPR's award-winning legal affairs correspondent. Her reports air regularly on NPR's critically acclaimed newsmagazines All Things Considered, Morning Edition, *and* Weekend Edition.

Viewpoint author Nina Totenberg discusses the 2012 Wisconsin congressional election, in which Democrats received considerably more votes but still lost seats. To many, this was a clear sign of gerrymandering. It was also one of the first times that computer algorithms had been used by the Republican Party to redraw districts based on voter analysis data. This tactic was spectacularly effective at winning seats for the Republicans, but its legality is currently being challenged in the Supreme Court. While computer algorithms could be used to draw democratic districts, the need for independent redistricting remains apparent. Totenberg argues that it is up to the Supreme Court to set a clearly defined legal definition for gerrymandering.

K eith Gaddie has "hung up his spurs."
The election expert from the University of Oklahoma no longer helps state legislatures draw new district lines to maximize their partisan advantage.

He was still wearing those spurs in 2011 when he provided data that helped Wisconsin Republicans enact a legislative redistricting plan aimed at maximizing their power for the foreseeable future.

But now he has reversed course and filed a brief in the US Supreme Court arguing that the practice is undemocratic.

The high court hears arguments Tuesday testing whether extreme partisan gerrymandering is unconstitutional. The case from Wisconsin has the potential to radically reorder politics in America.

In the short run, if the court sides with Gaddie, Republicans would be the losers. In the last two decades, the GOP has greatly increased and entrenched its dominance in the state legislatures and Congress through the use of partisan redistricting. The GOP now has control of state legislatures in 32 states, covering 61 percent of the population, while Democrats control just 13 state legislatures, covering 28 percent of the population.

What Is "Gerrymandering"?

Partisan gerrymandering is a practice that goes back to the early years of the republic. It got its name in 1812 when Massachusetts Gov. Elbridge Gerry signed into law a legislative map drawn to benefit his own party; it included a district so misshapen that it looked like a salamander, and the term gerrymander was born.

Since then, politicians from both parties have practiced, denounced and embraced it as a way to leverage their power. In 2004, the Supreme Court, by a 5–4 vote, refused to outlaw the practice. But the fifth and decisive vote was cast by Justice Anthony Kennedy, who left the door open to revisiting the issue if a manageable test could be found for evaluating how much is too much partisanship.

What This Case Is About

Now the issue is back in the case from Wisconsin, where Republicans in 2011 controlled both the legislature and the governorship in a redistricting year for the first time in decades, presenting them with a unique opportunity for consolidating their power.

Working in secret, they drew new district lines that would, for the remainder of the decade, solidify their control. A week after the plan was unveiled, the GOP majority enacted it into law.

The plan was amazingly on target. In the next election in 2012, Republicans, carried only a *minority* of the state vote—48.6 percent—but, as the GOP map designers had privately predicted, Republicans still won close to two-thirds of the state assembly seats, a 60–39 seat majority.

The tools the map designers used were not new—packing large concentrations of Democratic voters into a district to give the opposition party far more voters than they needed to win. They then spread out the remaining Democrats into districts where they would be clearly outnumbered (a practice known as cracking).

The Marriage of High Tech and New Data Analysis

A divided federal court found that while these techniques were not new, something else was—specifically, high-speed computer technology able to spit out thousands of alternative maps that meet the test of having equal numbers of residents and instantly matching each prospective map with new kinds of voter data to project outcomes well in advance of any election—all with breathtaking accuracy.

Gaddie emphasizes that he didn't draw any maps himself. What he did was create ways to run thousands of computer simulations, analyze the data and give it to those who actually were drawing the maps.

"They don't ask, 'Is this fair?'" Gaddie observes. "They just ask, 'What does this do?'"

Lawyers for the state say there are reasons for the Wisconsin district disparities that are *not* partisan.

"It is a political fact that Democratic voters tend to be relatively concentrated in urban areas and the Republicans are relatively dispersed in rural areas," said lawyer Paul Clement, who represents the GOP legislative leadership, none of whom wanted to be interviewed for this article.

Wisconsin Solicitor General Misha Tseytlin will defend the plan in the Supreme Court. He will tell the justices there is nothing salamander-like in his state's redistricting.

"It is undisputed," he contends, "that Wisconsin's map here complies with all traditional district criteria."

But the University of Michigan's Jowei Chen, an expert on geography and gerrymandering, has a different take. After running some 200 potential redistricting maps, he concluded that the state's demographic geography accounts for only one to three more seats for Republicans, whereas aggressively partisan gerrymandering yielded a 10 to 15 seat GOP advantage in the state legislature.

Moreover, Chen said, the heightened partisan advantage split more counties and municipalities than any of the sample, less partisan maps.

Is Extreme Partisan Gerrymandering Unconstitutional? Can the Courts Really Tell When a Plan Is Extreme?

The legal question before the Supreme Court is whether such partisanship in gerrymandering is so extreme that it is unconstitutional. Does it deny citizens the equal protection of the law; does it deny them their First Amendment right of free speech and association by making their votes less valuable? And ultimately is that something a court can accurately measure?

Lawyer Paul Smith, vice president of litigation and strategy at the nonpartisan Campaign Legal Center, represents those challenging the GOP redistricting plan. He will tell the justices the time has come for the court to act.

"There are now tests that were employed here to allow the courts to figure out what are the really bad gerrymanders," he said, adding that Wisconsin's is among the four worst partisan-drawn districts in the country.

The tests vary from a mathematical formula for measuring when districts are drawn to over-concentrate the voters of one party but not the other. There is also a broader and more conventional test for evaluating the degree of partisan redistricting, which was used by the lower federal court that first ruled in this case: 1. Was there discriminatory intent in drawing the districts? 2. Does the plan have a durable effect—will it entrench the same majority for the decade? And 3. Is there a neutral explanation for the way the lines are drawn, like the state's geography?

"When you have those three conditions, there ought to be a remedy," Smith said, "because what you have then is a sham of a democracy."

Election experts, including Gaddie, have filed briefs saying the technology now exists to answer these questions. But there are others who are not so sure. Among them is Princeton University's Nolan McCarty, who did not file a brief.

"I'm not saying that the Supreme Court shouldn't establish a principle against partisan gerrymandering, but I think it's going to be very hard to adjudicate in specific cases," he said. "Whether we can tell with any statistical precision whether or not a particular plan deviates from fairness in an illegal way is something that I'm a bit skeptical about."

Even Some Republicans Say the Supreme Court Should Act

Still, looking at the 53 amici curiae briefs filed in the case, 32 of them against partisan redistricting, it is striking how many Republicans, including current and former US senators, governors and state legislators, are urging the Supreme Court to act now to at least limit extreme partisan gerrymanders. They say these asymmetrical systems have grown so exponentially that they pose a threat to democracy.

Among those are two former GOP presidential candidates, Sen. John McCain of Arizona and former Sen. Bob Dole, former Oklahoma Gov. Frank Keating, former California Gov. Arnold Schwarzenegger and the former Assistant Republican leader of the US Senate Alan Simpson of Wyoming.

Never one to mince words, Simpson says of partisan gerrymandering, "It poisons the system.... It stinks!"

Less colorful, but equally firm is Republican Dale Schultz, who, for 32 years, served in the Wisconsin Legislature, rising briefly to the position of GOP leader. Schultz voted for the redistricting plan that is now before the Supreme Court, but he had second thoughts when he realized the enormous advantage it created for his party.

"The first big tipoff was after the [2012] election," he said, "when the Democrats had won a substantial victory in Wisconsin by, I think, 125,000 votes ... and lost a considerable number of seats in the legislature."

New tools to analyze voter behavior, "brought to bear with current technology amplifies what you can do in redistricting like we've never seen before," he added. "We've allowed technology and gerrymandering to sort of rob the people of their vote.... Legislators are picking their constituents rather than constituents picking their legislators."

Watch What You Wish For

Wisconsin Solicitor General Tseytlin, however, has a cautionary observation: "Not everything that one thinks is a bad idea is unconstitutional. We have a system where the courts have a certain bandwidth in which they can operate, and if there are no neutral principles that can be announced, it's better for the courts to stay their hand."

Supreme Court advocate Kannon Shanmugam agrees, voicing a further concern about the "inevitable politicization of the judiciary that's going to result" from "embroiling the courts in these quintessentially political disputes."

Some critics of court involvement point to an alternative solution adopted in some states: the creation of independent redistricting commissions to draw maps. At least seven states have adopted such commissions.

Most, however, were created by voter initiatives, over the objection of the state legislatures themselves, and only 11 states even allow such an initiative process according to the Campaign Legal Center.

A decision in the partisan gerrymandering case is expected later in the Supreme Court term.

9

Demanding a Solution to Gerrymandering Is the Responsibility of All Citizens

No Labels

No Labels is a social welfare advocacy organization dedicated to activating citizens and organizing leaders around a new politics of problem solving. It is working to build a durable bipartisan bloc in Congress.

Gerrymandering isn't the only issue in contemporary US politics. The nonprofit No Labels believes that political gridlocking is another tactic used by uncooperative representatives. Gridlocking is when politicians block or stall the political system to the point where political decisions cannot be made. Gerrymandering allows parties to fill the legislature with politicians who will toe the party line rather than enact the wishes of their constituents. No Labels believes gerrymandering and gridlocking can only be solved when citizens demand that their states use independent redistricting bodies. It is up to citizens to hold their representatives accountable for their political decisions.

G errymandering is best described by the origin of the word itself. It is believed to have been a combination of the last name of Elbridge Gerry, a governor of Massachusetts in the early 1800s, and the word "salamander." Why? Gov. Gerry signed into law a plan for dividing the legislative districts in his state that was intended to benefit his political party. One district was so misshapen a leading publication ran a cartoon showing how

"Just the Facts: Gerrymandering," No Labels, July 15, 2015. Reprinted by permission.

it resembled the winding shape of a salamander. For the next 200 years state legislatures have used their line-drawing powers to create strangely shaped districts to their political advantage.

Redistricting is a dry concept with large implications. Gridlock, dysfunction, and increasing polarization have all been in part attributed to how we draw our congressional districts. Each district altered for political gain has the potential to change—for the worse—how accurately our representatives reflect the views of the populace.

How Does Gerrymandering Work?

Gerrymandering often occurs in two forms, referred to as packing and cracking. Packing is when a legislature chooses to concentrate another group's members into one district, allowing the legislature's majority party to win all the others. Cracking, on the other hand, is breaking up that opposing party's bloc in order to make them the minority in many districts and unable to win elections. Both are strategic ways to give one party a better chance of holding more congressional and state legislative seats than they should win based on proportion of voters (gerrymandering also affects legislative districts).

Why Is Gerrymandering a Problem?

Gerrymandering is a way of cheating the system by creating an artificially positive balance of house seats for one party. For example, during the 2012 election cycle in Pennsylvania, 51% of the votes cast in the US House elections were for Democrats, yet the Democratic Party only won 5 out of 18 seats. If the majority of voters support one party, yet barely a quarter of representatives are a member of that party, it would appear there is disconnect between constituents and representation.

Not only does gerrymandering potentially skew voting, it is often argued that it contributes to polarization by advantaging more partisan candidates. An elected representative of a district that is 50% Democrat, 50% Republican will have to consider the needs of both halves of his or her constituents in order to be re-elected. If that same district were gerrymandered to be 80% Democrat, the representative can safely be partisan with no repercussions. While this system does not create partisanship and gridlock on its own, it certainly isn't one that fosters cooperation and compromise.

Is This Even Legal?

Every 10 years, in most states, the majority party controls the process of assessing the census results and deciding on districting. The Supreme Court has ruled that engaging in partisan gerrymandering is unconstitutional. However, proving in court that illegal redistricting has occurred is difficult; if a drawn district is reasonably contiguous and compact, there is little legal recourse.

The drawing of congressional district lines is the responsibility of the state legislature in 37 states. Seven states have only one representative, so districting policy is irrelevant. Only six states— Alaska, Arizona, Idaho, California, Montana and Washington— have independent commissions responsible for districting.

What Can We Do as Citizens to Make a Change?

In many states, citizens have passed referenda that require an independent agency to oversee or determine districting in their states. Recently, the Supreme Court upheld the right of citizens to use their legislative power to make such changes. Citizens can also advocate for a more transparent and public system within their states, so that elected officials are held accountable. While there is also support for the use of a program/algorithm that creates districting based on geography alone, ultimately it is the responsibility of the legislature to redistrict, and the citizens to alter their actions through referendum. Creating consistency in how districting occurs could eliminate uncertainty, and with oversight we can better assess and elect excellent candidates in every district.

Gridlock is a function of uncooperative representatives, and gerrymandering for political gain can be seen as a cause of this dysfunction. However, fixing our political system cannot stop at districting reform. Even if fixing the districting system was feasible today, it would only be a partial solution to the deep-seated problems in Washington. And the fact remains, for anything to be done, it will require many individual state-by-state slogs that can only occur every 10 years. We don't have time to wait for these battles to play out. We need solutions to gridlock now. By working within the system as it exists, rather than waiting for a better one, we can encourage candidates who are willing to compromise and cooperate across the aisle regardless of district lines.

10

Racial Gerrymandering Takes Many Forms

Lois Beckett and Suevon Lee

Lois Beckett has been a reporter for ProPublica since 2011. She covers the intersection of data, technology, and politics, with a current focus on gun violence and gun policy.

Suevon Lee was an intern at ProPublica. She has previously worked as a reporter for the Ocala Star-Banner, *where she covered courts and legal issues.*

Gerrymandering doesn't just happen along party lines: it happens along racial ones as well. The Voting Rights Act of 1965 included measures to prevent gerrymandering along racial lines. Unfortunately, in the early 2000s, it became clear that Texas was intentionally disenfranchising minorities. The tactic known as "cracking," which divides minority voters into separate districts, was intentionally employed to prevent minorities from having voting power. This was done at a time when minority voters were becoming the majority of the state's population. Authors Beckett and Lee describe the various other methods Texas politicians used while redistricting to disenfranchise minority voters.

Oral arguments begin today in a Supreme Court case challenging Section 5 of the Voting Rights Act as out of date. SCOTUS blog is reporting that "a majority of the Court seems committed to invalidating Section 5 of the Voting Rights Act."

"Five Ways Courts Say Texas Discriminated Against Black and Latino Voters," by Lois Beckett and Suevon Lee, ProPublica, Inc., February 27, 2013. Reprinted by permission.

In August, a panel of federal court judges ruled that new district maps drawn by Texas' Republican-controlled legislature weakened the influence of Latino voters and in some cases evinced "discriminatory intent" against both Latinos and African Americans. Two days later, another panel of federal judges unanimously struck down a voter-ID law passed by the legislature in March 2011, arguing that it would disproportionately harm African-American and Latino voters. The judges did not address whether there was discriminatory purpose behind the legislation, but they noted that the legislature failed to pass amendments that would have mitigated the law's discriminatory impact.

Both of these decisions hinged on Section 5, which requires certain states with a history of racial discrimination in voting—including Texas—to prove that any changes in their voting laws or procedures do not hamper the voting rights of minorities. Enacted in 1965, the Voting Rights Act aimed to eliminate discriminatory voting practices that had long been used to suppress the black vote, particularly in southern states.

In August, Texas Attorney General Greg Abbott's office declined to comment on the specifics of the rulings, but the state appealed both cases to the Supreme Court. Whether or not the Court will decide to hear Texas' redistricting case, which also challenges Section 5, may depend on how the court rules on the current Voting Rights Act case, *Shelby County v. Holder*.

Minority groups have outnumbered whites in Texas since roughly 2004, and 55.2 percent of the state's residents are now minorities, according to Census figures. But as of 2011, the state's legislature was more than two-thirds white.

Here's a look at examples of "discriminatory intent" and discriminatory impact federal judges found in Texas lawmakers' actions in 2011.

Lawmakers Drew Some Districts That Looked Like Latino Majority Districts on Paper—But Removed Latinos Who Voted Regularly and Replaced Them with Latinos Who Were Unlikely to Vote

In the redistricting case, a panel of three federal judges found that Texas lawmakers had intentionally created districts that would weaken the influence of Latino voters, while appearing to satisfy the requirements of the Voting Rights Act.

In drawing Texas' 23rd congressional district, the judges found that "the map-drawers consciously replaced many of the district's active Hispanic voters with low-turnout Hispanic voters in an effort to strengthen the voting power of [Congressional District] 23's Anglo citizens. In other words, they sought to reduce Hispanic voters' ability to elect without making it look like anything in [Congressional District] 23 had changed."

In 2010, the 23rd district narrowly elected a Latino Republican, Francisco "Quico" Canseco. One email to a Republican map-drawer, released during the legal battle over the maps, shows that Republicans were trying to increase the chances Canseco would be re-elected.

Lawmakers used a similar tactic in redrawing a state house district, modifying it "so that it would elect the Anglo-preferred candidate yet would look like a Hispanic ability district on paper," the court ruled. An "ability district" is one in which a minority group has the capability to elect representatives of its choosing. The judges concluded that the legislature had been trying to make this district appear as if it satisfied the requirements of the Voting Rights Act, while actually trying to benefit white voters.

Judge Thomas B. Griffith, writing the unanimous opinion of the three-judge panel of the US District Court for the District of Columbia, called it "a deliberate, race-conscious method to manipulate not simply the Democratic vote but, more specifically, the Hispanic vote."

Lawmakers Widened the Gap Between the Proportion of the Population That Is Latino and African Americans and the Proportion of Districts That Are Minority-Controlled

In the years leading up to the 2010 census, Texas' population increased by 4.3 million people, 65 percent of them Latino. As a result, Texas gained four seats in Congress.

In their decision, the federal judges in the redistricting case noted that minority voters have no constitutional right to proportional representation. But the Voting Rights Act says states can't weaken the electoral power of minorities. So, the judges reasoned, if there is already a gap between the minority population of a state and its political representation, states can't let that gap grow wider.

In Texas, the judges observed, African Americans and Latinos were already underrepresented in Congress. Given the number of voting-age minority citizens in the state, Texas' old maps should have had roughly 13 congressional seats that represent districts in which minorities have a strong voice, the judges calculated. Instead, Texas only had 10 such districts.

Instead of narrowing this "representation gap" as the minority population grew, the legislature increased it.

With four additional congressional seats, Texas should now have 14 districts in which minorities have the ability to elect their chosen representatives, the judges concluded. But the state's new plan still included just 10 minority districts.

Texas Removed Economic Centers and District Offices from African-American and Latino Districts, While Giving White Republicans Perks

In defending its new maps, Texas argued that the districts had been shaped to help Republicans and hurt Democrats—a perfectly legal tactic—and that race had been irrelevant to its choices.

The Associated Press reported that the state's lawyer had argued before the court that "'a decision based on partisanship' is not based on race, even if it results in minority voters having less political influence."

The judges noted that while there was no "direct evidence" that "discriminatory purpose" animated the new maps, circumstantial evidence indicated the design of the new congressional districts "was motivated, at least in part, by discriminatory intent."

Texas' gerrymandering was not limited to manipulating the kinds of voters within districts. By reshaping a district, map-drawers can determine whether key businesses, schools and tourist attractions are removed from a district or added to another.

The redistricting opinion dwelled at length on "unchallenged evidence that the legislature removed the economic guts from Black ability districts." African-American Rep. Al Green testified that the "economic engines" of his district—including a medical center, a university, and the Reliant Park sports mega-complex that includes the Astrodome—were removed. African-American Rep. Eddie Bernice Johnson's district lost a sports center and an arts district, while Latino Rep. Charles A. Gonzalez from San Antonio said that both a convention center and the Alamo were drawn out of his district.

These three members of Congress, and African-American Rep. Sheila Jackson Lee, all Democrats, also testified that their district offices were drawn out of their districts—a detriment because constituents want easily accessible district offices.

"No such surgery was performed on the districts of Anglo incumbents," the judges found. "In fact, *every* Anglo member of Congress retained his or her district office."

"The only explanation Texas offers for this pattern is 'coincidence.' But if this was coincidence, it was a striking one indeed," Judge Griffith wrote. He noted that Texas had argued that "without hearing from the members, the map-drawers did not know where the district officers were located." But, he wrote, "We find this hard to believe as well. We are confident that the map-drawers can not only draw maps but read them."

The judges noted that members of Congress who represented minority districts testified that they were largely shut out of the map-drawing process. At the same time, white Republican members asked for tweaks to their districts and were often accommodated. "Anglo district boundaries were redrawn to include particular country clubs and, in one case, the school belonging to the incumbent's grandchildren," the judges wrote, referring to requests related to the districts of Republican Congressman Lamar Smith, and Kenny Marchant, respectively.

Not all white lawmakers were happy with their new districts. Democratic Congressman Lloyd Doggett, who was forced to run in a new district as a result of the Republicans' maps, told the *Texas Tribune* last year that map plans "plunged a dagger into the heart of our community."

Divide and Conquer: Texas "Cracked" Minority Voters Out of One District into Three

One common tactic of racial gerrymandering is "cracking" a minority community into different districts so it cannot elect a minority politician.

Looking at a State Senate district in Fort Worth, the judges cited testimony that lawmakers reshaped the district in a way that "cracked the politically cohesive and geographically concentrated Latino and African American communities," and placed those voters "in districts in which they have no opportunity to elect their candidates of choice."

The judges cited "well supported" testimony that African Americans in Fort Worth had been "exported" into a rural, "Anglo-controlled" district to the South, while Latinos on the North side of the city had been put into another white, suburban district, leaving the "reconfigured" Senate District 10 a "majority Anglo" district.

The judges rejected Texas' argument that "its decision to 'crack' [Senate District] 10 is best explained by partisan, not racial, goals," and concluded that the district map "was enacted with discriminatory purpose."

Texas Passed a Voter-ID Law with Requirements That Would Make It Disproportionately Difficult for African Americans and Latinos to Vote

A three-judge panel found that Texas' voter-ID law discriminates against minorities, since the costs of obtaining the required identification would place a greater burden on low-income Texans, who are more likely to be minorities than white.

Although the state issues free election IDs, the cost of a birth certificate, one of the underlying documents needed for the ID, is $22—and that's if voters can get to the right government office in the first place. At least one-third of Texas' counties don't have a state Department of Public Safety office, which issues state IDs.

"It is virtually certain that these burdens will disproportionately affect racial minorities," wrote Judge David S. Tatel for the unanimous panel of the US District Court for the District of Columbia. He cited "undisputed US Census data" showing that Hispanics and African Americans in Texas are more likely to be poor and more likely to live in households without a car.

"Simply put, many Hispanics and Africans Americans who voted in the last election will, because of the burdens imposed by [the new voter ID law], likely be unable to vote in the next election," he wrote.

The judges agreed ahead of last month's trial to keep out any evidence indicating motivations for the voter-ID law, so they didn't address whether or not there was intentional discrimination behind the creation of the law. But the 56-page decision pointed out that the Texas legislature could have made its law more accommodating by, among other things, waiving documentation fees for the election IDs, reimbursing travel-related costs or expanding DPS office hours to evenings and weekends—amendments that were either defeated or tabled.

Finally, the judges agreed with Texas that the state had an interest in preventing voter fraud, even though there is little documented evidence of current voter fraud in Texas. However, they noted that circumstantial evidence "could nonetheless suggest that Texas invoked the specter of voter fraud as pretext for racial discrimination."

The 2012 Election

Texans were not required to present a photo ID to vote in November's election.

"As a result of the court's decision, Texas is not permitted to implement the photo ID law," Texas Secretary of State Hope Andrade announced in a news release.

As for the redistricting maps, Texas used a set of interim maps drawn by federal judges in Texas. Those interim maps were part of a contentious battle that earlier went to the US Supreme Court.

11

Prison-Based Gerrymandering Artificially Inflates the Population of Districts

Brenda Wright and Peter Wagner

Brenda Wright is the vice president of policy and legal strategies at Demos. She has led many progressive legal and policy initiatives on voting rights, campaign finance reform, redistricting, election administration, and other democracy and electoral reform issues and is a nationally known expert in these areas.

Peter Wagner is an attorney and executive director of the Prison Policy Initiative. He cofounded the Prison Policy Initiative in 2001 in order to spark a national discussion about the negative side effects of mass incarceration.

Authors Brenda Wright and Peter Wagner explain how prison-based gerrymandering is used to make the voting populations of districts seem larger than they actually are. This occurs because the census counts citizens as residents of the prison rather than of their home address. These census records are then used to create inaccurate districts because prisoners are not allowed to vote. In many states, people convicted of certain types of crimes, usually felonies, are not allowed to vote even after their sentence ends. Prison-based gerrymandering is sometimes used to create artificial minority-majority districts. Some states, like New York and Maryland, have passed laws to prevent this type of gerrymandering from taking place, and the viewpoint authors argue for the necessity of doing this.

Brenda Wright and Peter Wagner, "Preventing Prison-Based Gerrymandering in Redistricting: What to Watch For," Demos and Prison Policy Initiative, February 23, 2011.

P rison-based gerrymandering is the practice of counting incarcerated persons as "residents" of a prison when drawing legislative districts in order to give extra influence to the districts that contain the prisons. The US Constitution requires that election districts be roughly equal in size, so that everyone is represented equally in the political process. But prison-based gerrymandering distorts our democracy by artificially inflating the population numbers—and thus, the political clout—of districts with prisons, while diluting the political power of all other voters.

That this problem exists at all is largely an accident of two facts: (1) an outdated Census Bureau methodology that counts people in prison as residents of the correctional facilities, not of their legal home addresses; and (2) the skyrocketing rates of incarceration. Hopefully, in the future, the Census Bureau will eliminate the problem by counting incarcerated people as residents of their legal home addresses. Last year, three states—Maryland, Delaware and New York—had the foresight to pass legislation to eliminate prison-based gerrymandering within their borders. These three states now require that districts be based on Census data adjusted to reflect incarcerated people at their home addresses. More than a hundred rural counties and municipalities around the country have historically refused to engage in prison-based gerrymandering; they manually remove prison populations prior to drawing districts for local government. But most states and jurisdictions will still face the problem of prison-based gerrymandering in the upcoming round of redistricting.

When your legislature announces a proposed redistricting plan and invites public comment, you'll need to act quickly to identify if and exactly how they used prisons to distort democracy in your state, county or city. This guide will tell you what to look for in the data and the state's proposed plan in order to minimize the harm of prison-based gerrymandering.

Protecting Minority Voting Strength

Sometimes, a district that seems to have a majority-minority population really doesn't, because of prison-based gerrymandering. If the minority "population" of the district consists of large number of incarcerated persons—who can't vote—the district population numbers may be distorted. This creates districts that appear to give minorities the ability to elect the candidate of their choice, but in reality, they cannot. You need to examine any majority-minority district that includes a prison, to ensure that the district really has enough *voting-eligible* persons of color to create a viable majority with the ability to elect a candidate of choice to office.

Example: In order to settle a Voting Rights Act lawsuit, Somerset County Maryland intended to draw a district where African-Americans could elect a candidate of their choice after the 1990 and 2000 Censuses. But the inclusion of a large prison in the 1st Commission District split the sizable African-American resident voting population between two districts, leaving neither district able to elect a candidate of the African-American community's choice. While the 1st Commission District appeared to be majority-African-American, in reality the district was not able to function as intended, because many of the purported African-American "residents" of the district were actually behind bars.

Similarly, although to different effect, prison populations sometimes create a false picture of racial and ethnic "diversity" within a district. Pointing out these examples is an effective way to raise the issue of prison-based gerrymandering and can be a powerful fact to raise if, as discussed in the next section, the state has under-populated districts that contain prisons.

Example: District 2B in Western Maryland drawn after the 2000 Census appears to be 15% African-American. But nearly all of that African-American population actually consists of incarcerated residents from other parts of the state who are unable to vote or to interact with the community in any way. The actual population of the district is overwhelmingly white.

Example: In 2002, the New York State Senate deliberately underpopulated districts in the upstate region while overpopulating districts in the downstate region. This problem ran parallel to the fact that the Census Bureau credited downstate residents to upstate census counts, and together served to dilute minority voting rights. For example, one of those upstate districts was the 59th Senate District, drawn to contain 294,256 people instead of the 306,072 that each district should have contained. Using Census data, the state reported that the district contained 6,273 African Americans, but three quarters of this population was incarcerated residents of other parts of the state. The legislature used the prison population to disguise the fact that the district had the smallest African-American population of any senate district in the state *and* they deliberately underpopulated that district to give it extra influence.

Keeping Prison-Based Gerrymandering from Making Other Malapportionment Issues Worse

Advocates should examine what percentage of each district is actually incarcerated, and how that interacts with the existing population deviations in the proposed districts. Keep in mind that in the strange world of redistricting, "underpopulated" districts have more political power than "overpopulated" districts, because in underpopulated districts, fewer people get the same opportunity to elect a representative as a larger number of people crowded into an "overpopulated" district. For that reason, a district that nominally falls within the 5% deviation rule applicable to state and local districts, but would fall outside that deviation without the prison population, should raise a red flag, and should be examined carefully to determine if the deviation should be reduced. Apart from that specific situation, any districts having large prisons should be scrutinized to avoid underpopulation of such districts compared to ideal district size, because including prison population magnifies the underpopulation of the district.

Note that the inverse is also a concern, even if we don't have precise block-level data about the pre-incarceration home residence of people in prison who are currently being counted as "residents" of prisons. For example, you can use the fact that incarcerated people should have been counted at home to argue against extreme overpopulation of urban districts where incarcerated people disproportionately come from.

Limiting the Vote Enhancement in Districts with Prisons

Advocates should consider whether, if insufficient time remains to collect the home addresses of incarcerated people for this round of redistricting, the legislature can be persuaded to declare all incarcerated people to live at "unknown addresses" and not include them in the individual districts that contain prisons.

If the legislature will not consider removing the prison populations from individual districts, advocates should examine ways to limit the magnitude of the vote enhancement to each district that contains a prison. Advocates should determine what percentage of each proposed district is actually incarcerated, and consider whether it is possible to configure the districts so that multiple large prisons are not concentrated in an individual district, thereby lessening the size of the vote enhancement in the prison districts. Similarly, if a single block contains a massive prison, advocates should consider whether the block could be split in two, so that the prison population can be placed in two different districts, thereby lessening the vote enhancement in any one district.

12

Having More Political Parties Makes For More Competitive Elections

The Green Party

The Green Party is a left-wing political party in the United States. It promotes environmentalism, nonviolence, social justice, participatory grassroots democracy, gender equality, LGBT rights, pacifism, and racial equality.

One of the biggest problems with gerrymandering is that it leaves many people unhappy with their political representation. Most democratic nations have a number of political parties. This means there is more competition and voters have more options when it comes to representation. However, in the United States only two parties have real political power, which the Green Party argues is detrimental to American democracy. Third parties like the Green Party offer voters someone to vote for who fits somewhere between the dichotomy of the two major political parties. In the United States, alternative parties are often purposely shut out of things like televised debates and sometimes kept off ballots entirely, which the Green Party claims results in unfair elections.

Why a Third Party?

For one thing, third parties can force progress on political issues. The American political system contained many vigorous and powerful third parties throughout the late 18th and 19th centuries.

"Fix Our Broken System," the Green Party of the United States. Reprinted by permission. http://www.gp.org/fix_our_broken_system.

They forced the major political parties to pass significant anti-monopoly legislation back then, among other things.

The Presence of Viable Alternatives Keeps Americans Involved in Our Democratic Process

These third parties did more than simply force the two major parties to adopt various policies. Third parties have always provided an "emotional bridge" for voters who are weary of supporting one major party but are not yet ready to vote for the other. George Wallace's 1968 third-party presidential campaign drew support from traditional southern Democrats who weren't emotionally prepared to vote as Republicans.

[...]

Fix Our Broken System

If voting didn't matter, they wouldn't try so hard to keep you from doing it!

Our political system features numerous anti-democratic policies that are specifically designed to prevent the most oppressed sectors of our society from participating in the electoral process. Students and young people, African-Americans, poor people, and the elderly all face tremendous barriers, such as voter ID laws, disenfranchisement of ex-offenders, and restrictive residency requirements, among others. All Americans are affected to some degree by these policies, and our entire society suffers as a result.

Although political change is never easy to achieve, the fact that most election law is made at the state and local level is an opportunity. Organizers can develop and promote solutions locally that are much harder to achieve on a federal level.

> Everyone deserves the opportunity to influence the governmental decisions that affect them. But the defining characteristics of modern politics in the United States are a corrupt campaign finance system that enables corporate and wealthy elites to purchase political outcomes; and an abundance of anti-democratic electoral, ballot access and debate rules designed to minimize participation and choice.

The failure to fulfill the promise of democracy leaves millions of people in our country too discouraged to vote, and others who choose to vote seemingly trapped among false and limited choices. A system that promotes full and fair representation would draw millions of people in the United States into civic life and could revive democracy in this country.

—from the Green Party platform

Level the Playing Field
Ballot Access Reform

Ballots exist so that voters can choose who they want. But our ballot access laws actually TAKE AWAY voters' choices.

The US has made some progress over the years in enfranchising citizens who had been denied the right to vote, such as women, blacks, and poor people. However, we have been going backward when it comes to ensuring that, once someone has a ballot in hand, they are able to use that right to vote for someone they actually support. There are a number of reasons for that. However, the most basic reason, and probably the one people are least aware of, is our ballot access laws.

In the 1896 general election, every single congressional district in the nation had at least two candidates on the ballot. The average district had 3.1 candidates on the ballot. Today many Congressional incumbents and candidates have no opposition at all, as do many down-ballot candidates. The modern-day voter's choice is even more limited in state legislative races. In 2012, about one-third of all state House and Senate candidates ran unopposed.

Our ballot access laws are so bad that even Democrats and Republicans can't field candidates in quite a few races. However, these laws generally place far more restrictions on third parties.

Very few people are aware of the ballot access problem in the United States. Each state writes its own ballot access laws, even for federal office. Since there is no single standard for the whole nation, the public and even the media are ignorant about ballot access laws. By contrast, the campaign spending laws (for federal office) are uniform for the entire nation, leading to campaign spending laws for federal office being familiar to the press and most political activists.[1]

US Restricts the Ballot Far More Than Other Countries
The extreme disparity of the burdens placed on new parties vs. old, established parties in the US has no parallel in any other democratic nation in the world.

In Britain, for example, every candidate for Parliament faces the same ballot-access hurdle—a simple filing fee. Candidates, regardless of their party affiliation, are granted two free mailings to all the voters, and every candidate gets a certain amount of free TV and radio time. There exists legal equality between all the parties. None of these things are true for US candidates.

Unfortunately, the US Supreme Court has a rather erratic record when it comes to decisions regarding the constitutionality of ballot-access laws. While the court has, on occasion, upheld challenges to restrictive requirements, it has at other times ignored these same decisions.[2]

Ballot Access Has Gotten Worse Over Time
Originally, there were no ballot access restrictions whatsoever in the US. The government had no control over who could run for office, or whom voters could vote for. This is because, before the 1890s, the government didn't print the ballots! Instead, parties printed them and distributed them, and any voter was free to make his own ballot or to alter a party-printed ballot.

As recently as 1930, no state required more than 14,680 signatures for a new political party to get on the ballot.

Today, some states require huge numbers of signatures and/or votes for third parties to gain ballot access, while other states are much more reasonable. The laws vary enormously, not only in difficulty, but in the types of requirements they include, from state to state. This creates tremendous challenges for a third party trying to present an alternative and build an organization across the whole country.

For example, the two states that require support from the greatest number of supporters to get on the ballot are North Carolina and Oklahoma.[3] These states are far from the most populous states, and their barriers are all but impossible to overcome.

NC, with a population of about 9.8 million, requires almost 90,000 signatures. OK, with a population of about 3.8 million, requires more than 65,000. By contrast, New York, with almost 20 million people, and California, with 38 million, only require 50 to 60,000 supporters. NY requires 50,000 votes in the governor's race; CA requires 58,000 registered members.

Do We Need Ballot Access Restrictions?
Defenders of the restrictions say that candidates who lack substantial support must be kept off the ballot. Yes, some requirements are needed to keep the ballots from being clogged with too many candidates, but the very slightest ballot access barriers are sufficient for this purpose. In 1984, Tennessee only required 25 signatures for an independent candidate to get on the ballot for any office, and no fee was required: there were no independent candidates for the US House on the Tennessee ballot. It's a myth that there are dozens of people who want to run for office.

Open Debates
Voters learn about candidates through various sources: advertising, editorial coverage in the media, endorsements and personal contact. Debates are considered an extremely important part of this mix. Debates are often the only chance voters have to compare candidates side by side, and see them respond to questions in real time. Popular incumbents try to avoid them. Challengers push for them. Voters generally want to see more of them, and want more candidates to be included.

For third party candidates, who typically don't get much media coverage and can't compete with the major parties' ad budgets, debates are everything.

But the two major parties generally control debates. Not only do they do everything in their power to keep meaningful issues from being addressed, they try mightily, and usually succeed, in keeping third party candidates out.

[…]

Campaign Finance Reform
Money in Politics: The Sad State of Affairs
Today, new forms of big money undermine American democracy. Citizens United and other court rulings obliterated a century of campaign finance laws. Now a handful of special interests threaten to dominate political funding, often through Super PACs and shadowy nonprofits. Public trust in government has plummeted.[5]

The drive to allow ever-larger campaign contributions rolls on to what seems like new heights of absurdity, everywhere you look. The "Cromnibus" must-pass spending bill that went to Congress in December 2014 included (on page 1,599 of 1,603, and never mentioned in public before) a ten-fold increase in the amount of money people can give to party committees.

The legislation allows a single individual to contribute to each national party's three committees a total of $777,600 per year or $1,555,200 per two-year election cycle. It allows a couple to contribute to these committees a total of $1,555,200 per year or $3,110,400 per two-year cycle.

One-tenth of one percent of all tax returns in 2011 showed income of a million dollars or more (about 235,000 people). So there are very few people who could possibly hit these new campaign contribution limits.

Only two-tenths of one percent of all Americans donate to Federal campaigns at all.

[…]

Give Everyone a Voice
If voting didn't matter, they wouldn't try so hard to keep you from doing it!

Various representatives of the 1% never tire of trying to expand (not just maintain) their stranglehold on our entire political system, as well as our elected officials and other aspects of government, such as regulatory agencies and the courts.

Their effort has many tentacles and facets, from partisan redistricting to felon disenfranchisement and much more. At the same time, there are many Americans working tirelessly on behalf of the people, to reform the system and beat back attempts to take away our rights. The Green Party supports these efforts, on behalf of all Americans, not just our own members and supporters. Everyone deserves a voice in a democracy.

Fair Voting: No More "Lesser of Two Evils"

Have you ever felt forced to vote for the "lesser of two evils" even though you hated both candidates? Have you ever felt that voting for a Green whose values you share would "spoil" the election by helping elect a right-wing candidate? If so, this is the area of electoral reform that most directly addresses your problem.

Three's a crowd in our winner-take-all, plurality voting system. When there are more than two candidates, someone can win even though they didn't get the majority of the votes, only a "plurality" (more than anyone else). For example, in New York City Council primary elections, there are often six or seven candidates, and winners are declared with as little as 25% support.

By discouraging new candidates and parties, plurality voting suppresses new ideas and dissenting opinion. It encourages campaigns built around negative attacks.[4]

The good news is that fixing these problems doesn't mean embracing some "pie in the sky," crazy ideas that have never been tested. The US system, far from being the norm, is actually an outlier. *Nearly all* major, well-established democracies around the world use "fair voting" systems that allow voters to be much better represented than the American system does. There are also a number of American cities that use "fair voting" systems successfully, not to mention many non-political organizations.

Fair voting can refer to a range of voting methods in which "like-minded voters" (more on that later) elect candidates in proportion to their share of the vote. We will focus on those methods that would be easiest and quickest to achieve in the American context.

Proportional Representation

Proportional Representation depends on having at least some multi-member districts or at-large voting, where seats can be apportioned according to the percentage that different parties (or groups of like minded voters) achieve.

For example, in Peoria, IL, there is a ten-member City Council. Five members are elected, each from one of five districts in a "winner take all" election (whoever gets the most votes, wins).

The other five members are elected "at large," not representing a district, but the city as a whole. Each voter in the city gets five votes in the "at large" election. The top five vote getters are elected. This way, communities of interest across the city can get together to elect representatives. For example, if African-Americans, a minority of voters, coalesced around one candidate, each person could cast multiple votes for that one candidate and ensure that they had at least that one representative. This is known as "cumulative" or "bullet voting."

In the German Bundestag (comparable to our House of Representatives), they have a similar system ("mixed-member proportional representation"), but it is party-based. Half of the members of the Bundestag are elected directly from 299 districts. The other half are elected from party lists.

Accordingly, each voter has two votes in the elections to the Bundestag. The first vote, allowing voters to elect their local representatives to the Bundestag, decides which candidates are sent from the districts.

The second vote is cast for a party; it determines the relative strengths of the parties represented in second half of the Bundestag seats. The party determines the order that candidates will be seated in, depending on how many seats total the party wins.

In the Bundestag 2013 election, five parties gained seats.[7] Like-minded parties form coalitions within the Bundestag (the largest one becomes the governing coalition). Imagine how different our Congress would be, if different political strands were each represented with their own party, instead of fighting for a voice within a larger party, and they had to join with other parties in order to govern.

While there are some examples of proportional representation locally in the US, both currently and in the past, for the most part our system is made up of "winner take all" single-seat districts.

Instant Runoff Voting (IRV): It's as Easy as 1-2-3

IRV is a "fair voting" option for single-seat races. IRV allows all voters to vote for their *favorite* candidate, while avoiding the fear of helping elect their *least favorite* candidate. IRV allows "third parties" to compete in elections without losing potential supporters to the fear of "spoiling." It could demonstrate the TRUE level of support for the Green Party and our issues, helping us build power to enact our political agenda.

Compared to traditional runoff elections, IRV saves tax dollars spent on unnecessary elections, ensures winners have broader support than plurality elections, and elects winners when turnout is highest, rather than in separate run-off elections where turnout is typically extremely low.

IRV is used in local elections in Cambridge (MA) and some local offices in Minneapolis (MN), among other spots in the US.[5]

IRV allows voters to *rank candidates in order of preference* (i.e., first, second, third, fourth and so on). Voters have the option to rank as many or as few candidates as they wish. If no candidate gets a majority on the first round, a series of "runoffs" are simulated, using voters' preferences as indicated on their ballots.

After the vote, first choices are tabulated. The candidate who receives the *fewest* first choice rankings is eliminated.

All ballots are then re-tabulated, with each ballot that ranked the now-eliminated candidate first, now counting as a vote for that voter's SECOND choice.

The weakest candidates are successively eliminated, and their voters' ballots are added to the totals of their next choices.

Once the field is reduced to two, the candidate with the majority of votes wins.[6]

EXAMPLE: If IRV had been in place for the Presidential election of 2000, Green voters could have voted for Ralph Nader #1, and Al Gore #2. When Nader was eliminated, their votes would have transferred over to Gore.

The Green Party platform on these issues: Enact proportional representation voting systems for legislative seats on municipal, county, state and federal levels.

Enact Instant Run-off Voting (IRV) for chief executive offices like mayor, governor and president and other single-seat elections.

Nonpartisan redistricting

The Green Party platform on this issue: Establish independent and transparent non-partisan redistricting processes to stop partisan gerrymandering and protect minority rights and representation.

America's reliance upon winner-take-all elections and single-member districts (which most democracies around the world don't have)[7] has left our voting process open to the abuses of unfair partisan gerrymandering (unfairly drawing election districts at every level, local, state and congressional). Elected officials and their political cronies have used partisan redistricting to choose their voters, before voters have had the opportunity to choose them.[8]

If you look at most districts on a map, they have odd shapes, cutting out certain blocks, including narrow swaths of land across many miles, and so on.

The reason for these odd shapes is the creation of districts that have strong majorities of Republicans or Democrats, and in some cases, majorities or carefully blended mixes of certain ethnic groups. They have nothing to do with any actual communities, such as neighborhoods or even cities, and everything to do with favoring particular election outcomes.

Redistricting historically happened every ten years after the new census was released. Often, districts for a legislative body are supposed to each contain roughly the same number of people. For example, each district in the US House of Representatives represents approximately 700,000 people. So when the census comes out and it shows that populations have shifted from one place to another, the districts need to be re-drawn.

Now, as the process has become even more partisan, certain states like Texas have decided to re-draw districts every time a new party takes power in the state legislature, even if it is between census periods.

The creation of these non-competitive districts depresses voter turnout because voters feel they don't have a choice. Often, it means that voters LITERALLY don't have a choice. The dis-favored party doesn't even bother to run a candidate and the incumbent is unopposed.

FairVote notes that redistricting reform can *minimize* the ability of partisan legislators to punish their enemies and reward their friends. But for *truly competitive elections*, legislative diversity, and other public interest goals to be met, multi-member districts with proportional voting are needed to maximize the effectiveness of these reforms—and ensure all voters have choices, and no strong prospective candidate is shut out of a chance to participate.[9]

Other Electoral Reform Issues

There are many, many other aspects of our political system that could be improved, allowing more candidates to compete, and giving more citizens a real choice at the ballot box.

The nonpartisan Election Protection coalition was formed to ensure that all voters have an equal opportunity to participate in the political process . The coalition includes more than 100 local, state and national partners, such as the NAACP, ACLU, and Brennan Center for Justice. During elections, the coalition mobilizes thousands of volunteers to document election irregularities from the perspective of the voter. At all times, the coalition works on other election-related issues.

Here is a summary of a few of the key issues, adapted from the Election Protection website, 866ourvote.org.[10]

Voter Registration

Some states have begun making it harder for people to register to vote, often in the name of preventing voter fraud. Voter registration systems kept more than two million people from voting in 2008.

States have also begun to create new restrictions on voter registration drives.

There are also aggressive "purge" campaigns, which occur when states remove voters from the voter rolls. When the process is not done properly, duly registered voters can end up being purged.

There is always some kind of residency requirement, and each state is empowered to create its own definition of "resident." Residency requirements are particularly troublesome for college students. Some jurisdictions attempt to restrict college students' ability to vote at their campus address, and/or by absentee ballot when away at school. Some actively try to deny students' right to vote. For example, students at Georgia Southern University (GSU) in Statesboro, GA, were falsely told that they would risk losing their financial aid, and that their parents could no longer claim them as dependents on their tax returns if they voted there.

Many issues impact voter registration like inadequate resources, clerical errors and failures to notify registrants of problems with their registration forms in a timely manner.

Some solutions:

- Election Day or Same Day registration
- Online registration
- Voter Registration Modernization (VRM)—VRM will automatically register every eligible American to vote when

they turn 18 or become citizens. Additionally, when voters move, their registration will move with them.

- Early and absentee voting
- Many voters may not be able to vote in-person at the polls on Election Day, whether because they have work obligations, are out of town, or cannot physically get to the polls because of a disability or lack of ready access to transportation. States have adopted early voting to provide these voters with a better opportunity to cast a ballot.
- Absentee Voting: All states allow absentee voting so voters can submit ballots by mail on or before Election Day.
- Early Voting: Voters can vote early in thirty-two states and the District of Columbia. Available hours and locations vary (and the right wing has sued to restrict early voting options in some places).

[...]

Voter ID/Proof of Citizenship

The right-wing group ALEC (American Legislative Council) has made it a high priority to get voter ID laws passed all over the country.

According to the Brennan Center, since the 2010 election, new voting restrictions are slated to be in place in 22 states. (These include voter ID laws, restrictions on early voting, and other issues.) Unless these restrictions are blocked—and there are court challenges to laws in six of those states—voters in nearly half the country could find it harder to cast a ballot in the 2014 midterm election than they did in 2010.[11]

All states require an individual to be a US citizen in order to vote in state or federal elections. Each state requires its residents to provide some form of ID to vote, which varies by state. In the least restrictive states, residents only need to have their signature verified.

In the most restrictive states, individuals must present a government-issued photo ID and individuals unable to produce the required ID are not allowed to vote. In Indiana, the single most restrictive state, the photo ID must be issued by the State of Indiana or the United States, it must bear an expiration date that has not elapsed, and it must contain the voter's name in a manner that conforms to the voter's registration record.

It's hard to even imagine how many voters could be disenfranchised by that final requirement, if a middle initial were included or excluded, or a name were slightly misspelled.

Proof of citizenship and voter ID requirements impact all voters, but fall more significantly on traditionally disenfranchised groups including poor, minority and elderly voters.

Deceptive Practices

Deceptive practices are the dissemination of false or misleading information about elections and the voting process in order to alter the outcome of the election and to prevent eligible voters from casting their ballots. In most cases, deceptive practices target traditionally disenfranchised communities—including minorities, seniors, and young people—and very rarely are the perpetrators pursued or prosecuted by law enforcement.

Often, deceptive practices take the form of flyers or robocalls giving false information to voters about the time, place and manner of elections. Recently we have seen more sophisticated and nuanced tactics like using text messages, emails, Facebook posts and messages on Twitter attempting to deceive voters.

In order to effectively combat these fraudulent election practices, we need stronger laws. Deliberately deceiving voters about any aspect of the voting process should be unambiguously illegal. Federal, state and local officials should be empowered not just to punish violators, but also to quickly correct deceptive information through sources trusted by affected communities.

References
1 BALLOT ACCESS: A Formidable Barrier to Fair Participation, by Richard Winger

The Battle to Get on the Ballot

http://web.archive.org/web/20110611145451/http://www.ballot-access.org/winger/fbfp
.html

2 "The Importance of Ballot Access," by Richard Winger. Reprinted with permission from the Spring 1994 Long Term View, Massachusetts School of Law, Andover, MA.

http://web.archive.org/web/20110611123629/http://www.ballot-access.org/winger/iba.html

3. "California Governor Signs Bill, Easing Rules for New Parties to Get on Ballot and Existing Parties to Remain on the Ballot," September 30, 2014, by Richard Winger

4. FairVote website, accessed 11/27/14.

5. FairVote website, accessed 11/4/14.

6. Adapted from FairVote website, accessed 11/27/14.

7. More on winner-take-all and single-member-districts later.

8. FairVote website, accessed 11/3/14.

9. FairVote website, accessed 11/3/14.

10 Election Protection website, http://www.866ourvote.org, accessed 11/27/14.

11. http://www.brennancenter.org/analysis/state-voting-2014

13

Voter Apathy Caused by Gerrymandering Leads to Low Voter Turnout

Shannon Sabo

Shannon Sabo is the marketing director at William S. Hein and Co., Inc. and HeinOnline.

Gerrymandering may seem like a new tactic, but it's actually as old as America itself. Since the first congressional elections, politicians have attempted various methods to sway the results in their favor. Viewpoint author Shannon Sabo claims that one of the most difficult-to-combat effects of gerrymandering is public apathy toward elections. When elections are heavily gerrymandered, many voters begin to feel that their vote will have no effect. This leads to lower voter turnout. When voter turnout is low, the number of voters politicians need to win is smaller and far less representative. Sabo argues that the best way for citizens to combat this effect is to make sure they vote.

G errymandering has been around since the election of the first US Congress. The concept has received more attention recently, as the unexpected results of the 2016 election have placed a spotlight on the US government and the processes of democracy generally.

"A Brief and Reptilian History of Gerrymandering," by Shannon Sabo, HeinOnline, July 12, 2017. Reprinted by permission.

What's Gerrymandering? Was There Really a Gerry Mander?

Gerrymandering is the process of manipulating election district boundaries to favor one political party over another, often leading to underrepresentation of the actual majority of constituents.

Gerrymandering is problematic for several reasons:

- It undermines the principle of "one person, one vote."
- It contributes to "safe seats," where voters end up deciding which party wins but not who their representative actually is. In these instances, nominations may be decided by a minority of activists and can be heavily influenced by organized and moneyed interests.
- It contributes to low voter turnouts, as voters become apathetic when they feel their votes have no meaning.
- It contributes to the reputation of politics and democracy as "fixed" or corrupt.

The term gerrymandering was first used in 1812. The Governor of Massachusetts, Elbridge Gerry, signed a bill that redistricted Massachusetts to benefit his political party (which was called the Democratic-Republican party, in case this wasn't confusing enough). When mapped, one of the reorganized districts resembled the shape of a salamander, thus creating the term gerrymander.

Because politics and law frequently intersect, gerrymandering has been studied and written about extensively in academic and legal publishing.

14

Portions of the Voting Rights Act That Restrict Racial Gerrymandering Are in Jeopardy

Richard Valelly

Richard Valelly is the Claude C. Smith '14 Professor of Political Science at Swarthmore College.

The Voting Rights Act of 1965 was an attempt to end African American voter disenfranchisement. The law's creators understood that simply having the right to vote wasn't enough to counter years of systemic racism in the political system. For equality to be achieved, minorities needed to have a fairer shot at being elected. Some provisions in the Voting Rights Act were meant to make it easier for minorities to elect representatives. Unfortunately, lawsuits have been steadily chipping away at the power of the Voting Rights Act. Some hold the belief that efforts to ensure minorities have the same voting power as whites is discriminatory to white people. In this viewpoint, Richard Valelly explains why the Voting Rights Act matters and challenges the arguments against it.

A rumor has been coursing through the Internet and black talk-radio shows: Congress will disenfranchise black Americans when it reconsiders the 1965 Voting Rights Act—which it must do by no later than 2007. The Congressional Black Caucus has fielded hundreds of anxious phone calls over the past two years; the Justice Department now posts a Web site rebuttal.

"Voting Rights in Jeopardy," by Richard Valelly, the American Prospect, September-October, 1999. Reprinted by permission.

Such rumors illustrate that the "paranoid style" in American politics persists. Yet the Voting Rights Act is indeed under fire. In its inception, the act was structured to make sure black Americans could register and vote. But as techniques of resistance in the white South became more baroque, so did the act, its interpretation, and its remedies. To some critics, this shift signaled regulatory overreach and racial preference. And in the past decade, the use of racially conscious legislative districting to increase black representation has further stimulated political and judicial backlash. Today, political momentum has shifted to critics of the act, and a major rollback, either legislatively or through the courts, could well occur.

Massive Resistance

Prior to the Voting Rights Act of 1965, barriers to black registration and voting were massive and crude. The entire white southern way of life was at stake. It was voting rights, more than anything else, that stimulated the 1964 Freedom Summer, voting rights that split the 1964 Democratic National Convention, and voting rights for which young activists gave their lives. In 1964, Mississippi had only about 7 percent of its black voting-age population registered to vote, with a voting-age population that was 36 percent black, Alabama, with a voting-age population that was 26 percent black, registered less than one eligible black voter in four, and Louisiana, with a voting-age population that was 28 percent black, registered less than one in three. In 1964, out of about 29,000 local, state, and national elected officials in the entire ex-Confederacy of 11 states, just 16 such officials were black, 3 of these state legislators and 13 local officials.

The 1965 act focused entirely on the franchise. The act contained two sets of provisions, permanent sections that prohibited discrimination in voting, and temporary elements for enforcement, subject to renewal. The most important of these temporary features was Section 5 pre-clearance, which empowers the Justice Department to pre-clear any proposed changes in local registration and voting procedures. But there were also other temporary sections that barred specific impediments to voting and that provided for direct federal observation or examination of electoral processes as they occurred. This was the most basic takeover by Washington of local civic functions since Reconstruction; it was richly deserved and roundly resented.

No sooner was the law enacted than several southern state legislatures adopted programs of massive resistance to voting rights, much like the earlier massive resistance to school desegregation. States recast entire systems of representation in order to dilute black influence. They permitted or required county and municipal governments to create at-large voting for public offices, which submerged geographic black voting strength within a larger white majority. They changed balloting systems so that black voters were forced to vote for entire tickets, thus blocking any "single-shot" or "bullet-voting" by blacks for a liberal or minority candidate, which had been permitted previously in some jurisdictions. They pushed local governments to establish absolute majority vote requirements for winners, thus preventing plurality victory by a black candidate over a split field of whites. They converted elective offices to offices appointed by officials likely to have exclusively white support. Finally, states reapportioned legislative and congressional district lines to submerge black voting strength in white majorities.

With these changes, blacks could vote—but could achieve neither fair representation nor elective office. In 1969, however, the Supreme Court rejected such vote dilution in *Allen v. State Board of Elections*. Mississippi officials had defended a 1966 maneuver converting the district election of county supervisors to an at-large election, as was permissible under the Voting Rights Act. Since the act ostensibly covered only registration requirements, Mississippi's change had not required clearance from the Justice Department.

The Supreme Court, however, grasped the essential politics of the matter. If blacks could not elect county supervisors, the old local white power structure would survive intact. Traditional white elites would continue to levy county taxes and spend county money as before, directing construction and maintenance money to white contractors and white neighborhoods, appointing all-white welfare and planning boards without concern for minority interests, and drawing up white jury lists for the state courts.

The Court ruled that such devices did in fact require clearance. It held that the right to vote can be affected by a "dilution of voting power as well as by obstacles to casting a ballot. Voters who are members of a racial minority might well be in the majority in one district, but in a decided minority in the county as a whole. This type of change could therefore nullify their ability to elect the candidate of their choice just as would prohibiting some of them from voting."

With *Allen*, the burden of proof shifted to affected states and localities to show that proposed changes in electoral systems, as well as voting procedures, were not discriminatory. *Allen* thus made it possible for the Justice Department to efficiently monitor the evolution of state and local electoral structures. The Justice Department's Civil Rights Division has scrutinized about 200,000 proposed changes to electoral rules since *Allen* and objected to about 1 percent of them.

In a subsequent 1973 decision from Texas, *White v. Regester*, the Court further held such vote dilution unconstitutional under the 14th Amendment. Armed with *White*, the private voting rights bar was able to overthrow many at-large structures and gerrymanders that predated the Voting Rights Act, in some cases by half a century. Litigation also challenged vote dilution in places not explicitly covered by Section 5, including southwestern jurisdictions where Anglo politicians had long rigged systems of representation to short-circuit Latino political influence.

The *Allen* and *White* rulings and the concept of "dilution of voting power" were in effect codified in the 1982 amendments to the Voting Rights Act. Congress said that while nothing in the act "establishes a right to have members of a protected class elected in numbers equal to their proportion in the population," it also provided that there is a "denial or abridgement of the right to vote" if electoral processes are not "equally open to participation" by "members of a protected class" and if such members "have less opportunity . . . to elect representatives of their choice."

The Backlash

The entire anti-vote dilution movement of the past three decades, and the provisions of the Voting Rights Act supporting it, are now lightning rods for controversy. Critics such as Abigail Thernstrom see the anti-vote dilution approach as regulatory excess. She and kindred critics make three basic points. First, even in the Deep South, politics have sufficiently normalized to the point where heroic federal supervision of local affairs is no longer necessary. Second, anti-dilution measures, especially "racial gerrymandering," have gone too far and now amount to unconstitutional favoritism which violates the 14th Amendment. Third, liberal critics such as the political scientist Carol Swain argue that the herding of black voters into districts of their own has "bleached" surrounding districts, paradoxically leading to the overall election of more conservatives unfriendly to black interests.

Since the early 1990s, the Supreme Court itself has increasingly undermined the anti-vote dilution doctrine and program without explicitly reversing its earlier decisions. The Court has applied some of its long-held unease about affirmative action to the voting rights domain. A majority of the Court now holds that the equal protection clause of the 14th Amendment casts grave doubt on whether government efforts to aid minorities are any more defensible than government efforts to favor whites; ideally, government should be "color-blind." Four justices, Anthony Kennedy, William Rehnquist, Antonin Scalia, and Clarence Thomas, believe that all race-conscious policies—including voting rights policies—run some risk of being invidious. Racial classifications should therefore be subject to "strict" judicial scrutiny, and upheld only if there is a compelling interest in support of the classification. Otherwise, the policy denies equal protection of the laws.

Only the ambivalence of one justice has kept the Court from a major retreat on vote dilution. In key recent decisions, Justice Sandra Day O'Connor has sent mixed signals, leaving 30 years of anti-vote dilution law and politics under a cloud of constitutional suspicion. But there will likely be far less sympathy for the vote-dilution doctrine by the time the temporary provisions of the Voting Rights Act come up for statutory renewal in 2007.

Helms's Integrity

If the Supreme Court and/or Congress do substantially weaken the act, what then? The answer depends on how rational politicians with little attachment to minority interests will respond to a looser regulatory environment. Here the paradigmatic story is Jesse Helms's 1990 senatorial re-election campaign.

Recall that George Bush won the presidency in 1988 partly by savaging Willie Horton. His chief electoral strategist, the late Lee Atwater, used racial polarization to build the Republican Party. This was the national backdrop to events in North Carolina in the fall of 1990.

The Helms for Senate Committee and the North Carolina Republican Party arranged for 125,000 postcards to be mailed to black-majority voting precincts. The cards falsely stated that people who had recently changed residence would not be allowed to vote under North Carolina law, would be required to prove residence on election day, and risked federal criminal penalties of up to five years in jail if they gave false information. Two separate targeted mailings occurred after official voter registration figures showed that the percentage increase in African-American registration in the run-up to the election was twice that of white voters (10.6 percent, as opposed to 5.3 percent for whites). Polls also showed that Helms's African-American opponent, Democrat Harvey Gantt, was ahead eight points.

When thousands of postcards came back as undeliverable, the North Carolina Republican Party then began to draw up lists of voters who would be challenged on election day itself. The

Justice Department swung against this last effort, and the Helms campaign dropped it. In early 1992, the various defendants and the Justice Department signed a consent decree enjoining such ballot security programs. (Helms evidently misjudged the Bush administration. Its assistant attorney general for civil rights refused to tolerate Helms's "ballot integrity" program.) Whether a future Justice Department could move against a future ballot integrity strategy depends on how seriously Congress and the courts weaken the Voting Rights Act.

Rights in Jeopardy

The Voting Rights Act, as applied, has been in trouble with the Supreme Court since the *Shaw v. Reno* decision of 1993, in which the Court limited racial gerrymandering. The Court ruled that white plaintiffs in the Twelfth Congressional District of North Carolina were entitled to a full lower court trial to determine whether the North Carolina state legislature had created a majority-black congressional district so gerrymandered that it violated the equal protection clause. Then, in a 1995 Georgia case, *Miller v. Johnson*, the Court stated that race cannot be a "predominant factor" in congressional districting. But a year later, in a Texas case, *Bush v. Vera*, the Court's vital "fifth vote," Justice O'Connor, defected from the coalition she had built in *Shaw*. In her opinion for the Court, O'Connor explicitly stated that the states could not reasonably avoid taking race into account when they drew congressional districts. Indeed, strict scrutiny did "not apply to all cases of intentional creation of majority-minority districts."

For the second time in American history, the federal government might largely withdraw from enforcing black voting rights. This last happened in the mid-1890s, when the Democratic Party used the occasion of unified government during Grover Cleveland's second administration to repeal the federal election laws established during Reconstruction to enforce the 14th and 15th Amendments. In that vacuum of federal protection, black disenfranchisement accelerated between 1890 and 1910, as state constitutions were amended and legislatures instituted highly effective literacy tests and poll taxes. The great democratic experiment of Reconstruction expired. Shortly after, Congress and President Woodrow Wilson approved a thorough segregation of the federal workforce and of the government washrooms and lunchrooms in the District of Columbia. Symbolically, the federal government was now for whites only.

Of course, unlike in the 1890s, intense racism in electoral politics is now defunct. Both parties now compete for the votes of blacks, Hispanics, and Asian Americans. Further, even if racism persists, African Americans have political resources to take care of themselves—due in part to the Voting Rights Act itself. One of the architects of the act, Nicholas Katzenbach, emphasized this point in a recent interview (even as he characterized *Shaw* and *Miller* as "nutty decisions"). Every southern legislature has experienced black office holders. Many white politicians have large numbers of black constituents. The playing field in race relations may well be level enough to compensate for federal departure from electoral regulation.

Or is it? As an aphorism attributed to Mark Twain has it, "History may not repeat itself but it sure can rhyme." Here is how history might rhyme.

How History Might Rhyme (I)

First, minority voters might suddenly find the act of voting a bit more chilling. If Congress declines to renew the act's pre-clearance mechanism, then local governments could resort to a variety of tempting tactics. For instance, they would be free to relocate the polls to predominantly white schools in neighborhoods known for, say, aggressive policing. Such ploys occurred in the 1970s; are we sure they would not happen again?

Expiration of the act's special provisions would also end the federal observer and examiner mechanism. Crude, Jesse Helms-style "ballot integrity" programs could well produce lawsuits under the weaker 1957 and 1960 Civil Rights Acts. But even armed with the full statutory authority of the 1965 act as strengthened in 1975 and 1982, the feds did not smoothly swing into action against Helms's 1990 ballot security campaign. A former attorney at the Justice Department told me recently that it was a "Herculean task" to assemble a bureaucratic coalition for intervention. Most ballot integrity programs are more subtle, like the radio ads in a local Texas contest in the early 1990s that sought to confuse elderly black voters about whether their absentee voting was legal. Or they resemble New York City Mayor Rudy Giuliani's campaign against his predecessor, David Dinkins, in which city police officers placed posters in Hispanic neighborhoods announcing that noncitizens who voted would be subject to penalties by the Immigration and Naturalization Service.

With a weaker statute, most such maneuvers would fly below the Justice Department's radar, but still dissuade minority voting. The temptation is enormous, in a close election, to try some funny stuff to keep some minority voters away from the polls, particularly if the candidate has already written off minority support.

How History Might Rhyme (II)

There's a second way history could rhyme. Local governments with narrow white electoral majorities could return to at-large elections for city or county government. Or they could annex white suburbs or make other kinds of changes that produce vote dilution. But without Section 5 pre-clearance, the burden of proving discriminatory intent would shift to minority plaintiffs. Some changes might actually be immune from challenge at all. Earlier in this decade, the Eleventh Circuit Court of Appeals held that judicial elections were immune from vote dilution claims if a state argued that it had a compelling interest in having such elections be at-large. Obviously this could be a slippery slope toward more at-large elections.

[...]

In other words, a return to old-fashioned vote dilution could occur simply through shifting the odd, costly burdens of proof to minority plaintiffs. In a more permissive environment of a weaker act, the entire landscape of voting would be different. And all of this would be occurring in the context of dramatically altered public opinion.

In 1987—one year after a decision in which a friendlier Supreme Court explained how voting rights plaintiffs could implement the new, amended Section 2—the political scientist Abigail Thernstrom published an influential attack on the anti-vote dilution program. In *Whose Votes Count?*, she spelled out what she considered regulatory excess. Since her book appeared, several critical propositions about the Voting Rights Act have gained a wide audience.

First, as noted, the regulatory excess critique of the Voting Rights Act holds that special provisions for minority office-holding were unnecessary; black politicians would have done fine on their own. Critics such as Thernstrom concede that whites, especially in the South, seldom vote for black candidates. But for Thernstrom et al., black candidates do not lose among white voters because of racial animus, but because they are too liberal for most whites. These outcomes are policy quarrels, largely devoid of invidious racial meaning.

Yet in jurisdictions covered by the Voting Rights Act, the increases in black and minority office-holding in local and state legislatures and in Congress have depended on federal intervention. Two landmark studies, *Quiet Revolution in the South*, edited by Bernard Grofman and Chandler Davidson (1994), and J. Morgan Kousser's *Colorblind Injustice* (1999), have shown this unambiguously. Thernstrom's idea that minorities, absent federal intervention, would have gained office at anything like the same rate is pure fancy.

As Thomas Pettigrew, the sociologist, has put it in an oft-quoted passage, "If a black is running against a white, you look at survey data and you take the white 'don't know' vote and simply add it to the white candidate's total. Ten times out of ten that comes within a couple of percentage points of what happens." Verifying this estimate in an ingenious clinical experiment described in his recent book, *Voting Hopes or Fears?*, my colleague Keith Reeves empirically confirmed Pettigrew's educated guess.

So blacks do have some trouble gaining white support, and not just because there are policy disagreements. Again, this suggests that without the anti-vote dilution program of the past 30 years, there would be far fewer minorities in public office today.

Of course, there is more to the debate over the anti-vote dilution program. Many have noted a subtle problem with using the Voting Rights Act to get minorities into state legislatures and Congress: it seems to weaken the southern Democratic Party, as Carol Swain first pointed out some years ago. In order to have more minorities serving in the House, and thus to meet the requirements of the amended Section 2 of the Voting Rights Act, Democratic state legislatures armed with new, sophisticated software created ultra-gerrymandered districts in covered states. They did this in order to maximize black ability to elect black representatives, while doing minimal partisan damage to adjacent districts. Swain concluded, with some overstatement, that this process drained surrounding districts of minority voters. Implementing the Voting Rights Act "bleached" these districts, in other words. As Justice Scalia asked in 1995 during oral argument in a voting rights case, "Aren't the black community's interests better served if black voters are spread among many districts rather than concentrated in a few?"

In fact, the white South was well on the way to going heavily Republican with or without the creation of majority-minority seats. At most, the concentration of minority votes tipped a few additional seats into the Republican column. In addition, David Lublin, an American University political scientist, has performed a statistical analysis indicating that substantive representation of black interests "kicks in" when a district's voting-age population is around 40 percent black. In other words, "influence" districts of about 40 percent would have been good enough for black representation and even black office-holding, with less "bleaching" of surrounding districts. This finding should strengthen both the intellectual, political, and constitutional case for retaining race-sensitive districting.

Nonetheless, it remains the case that strong measures against vote dilution, including the deliberate creation of districts where blacks had a reasonable shot at winning election, were necessary to get minority politicians off to a running start. The representative from a congressional district which has a minority voting-age population below about 40 percent turns out to be more or less blind and deaf to minority policy interests.

It is certainly encouraging that minority office holders have been able to build multiracial coalitions, and to survive redistricting that deprived them of majority-minority districts. But this is entirely the fruit of the Voting Rights Act and the racially conscious districting that allowed them to attain office in the first place. We aren't going to get such politicians, however, without majority-minority districting in some form. Without it, there is less chance that we will see minorities at the legislative table, and out and about, working their districts, building multiracial cooperation.

In sum, the "regulatory excess" view of federal voting rights policies is a gross exaggeration. The "bleaching" argument is empirically much sounder, but it has been rather overblown. Majority-minority districting of congressional, state, and local districts builds social solidarity. It has, indeed, helped white voters in many congressional districts to trust minority office holders. There are alternatives to it, such as cumulative voting and proportional representation, and in principle they are attractive. But if campaign finance reform, a major issue, cannot make progress, it strains credulity to think that we will ever see a full-scale shift to electoral structures that voters would regard as genuinely foreign.

Back to Which Future?

Emerging trust in minority office-holding gets to the bottom-line issue: What kind of political future do we want? One future we might go back to is something like the gradual diminution of minority office-holding that happened in the 1880s and 1890s. The other future toward which we can go back is the rich experiment in representation and office-holding which this country pioneered during Reconstruction.

From 1867 to 1877 about 2000 blacks served as federal, state, and local office holders in the ex-Confederate states subject to congressional Reconstruction. They were almost all strongly Republican in their policy views, and concentrated in the Deep South states with majority black or significantly black populations: South Carolina, Mississippi, Louisiana, North Carolina, Alabama, and Georgia, in that order. Between 1868 and 1876 an average of 268 black men served during the legislative sessions of the state legislatures in 10 southern states.

The standard picture of Reconstruction, of course, is that it was a time of corruption and incompetence. In fact, minority office-holding meant good government—it meant public education systems that the South never had, America's first civil rights laws, and fair criminal justice as blacks sat on juries for the first time. In South Carolina there was a very brief period of decently administered, state-sponsored homesteading and land reform for black families. In the city of New Orleans minority office-holding meant the first genuinely integrated school system in America (and, unhappily, the last such system for a century). In several states, the legislatures also supported nascent trade unions and labor movements of, for instance, stevedores and rice pickers.

As it happens, we do not face an all-or-nothing decision of the kind imagined in rumors of disenfranchisement. A reversal of voting rights gains would be gradual and incremental. But rather than passively waiting to see what comes, we ought to positively renew our national commitment to the practices that once made America a pioneer in democratic possibility. We should keep working toward giving the 15th Amendment all of the meaning its framers wanted for it. With the civil rights laws of the 1960s we redeemed the Civil War amendments of the 1860s. But there is still work to do to make history rhyme the right way.

15

Proportional Elections and Independent Redistricting Efforts Are Both Needed to Make Elections Fairer

FairVote

FairVote is a nonpartisan champion of electoral reforms that give voters greater choice, a stronger voice, and a representative democracy that works for all Americans.

Having a winner-take-all two-party system means that, in many locations, citizens may not actually approve of either of their choices for representation. Groups like FairVote believe that elections should promote fair representation of race and gender while also ensuring that everyone's vote has equal power. This viewpoint reviews the ways gerrymandering affected the 2012 election cycle but argues that redistricting isn't the only solution. FairVote is one of many groups that believe proportional voting could help make elections more representative and democratic. By doing away with the winner-takes-all method of voting, districts would become more competitive and allow everyone a real chance to elect someone who accurately represents their views.

The lack of fairness and accountability in Congressional elections is drawing welcome attention. Democrats in the 2012 elections won only 46% of House seats despite winning more votes than Republicans. More than three out of five races were

"It's Not Just Gerrymandering: Fixing House Elections Demands End of Winner-Take-All Rules," Fair Vote, December 16, 2012. Reprinted by permission.

won by landslide margins of at least 20%, women remain deeply under-represented and the number of centrist and independent legislators declined again.

But most analysts overlook the real problem: the 1967 law mandating that states elect US House Members in single-member district, winner-take-all elections. A lack of voter choice, the distortion between voter intent and outcome, and the reduction of centrist legislators has relatively little to do with the redistricting process of 2011 compared with the very fact of districting itself. The fundamental cause of partisan bias in the House is that Democrats are relatively concentrated in urban areas, and the fundamental cause of the lack of voter choice in most elections is that most areas of the country have a clear partisan lean. Gerrymandering is problematic, but is not the root of our electoral dysfunction.

Confronting the reality that winner-take-all rules are at the heart of the problems with our elections points us to the only reform solution: the adoption of fair voting systems. These American forms of proportional representation are based on voting for candidates in larger districts with more than one representative. By allowing like-minded voters who make up 20% of the vote to elect at least one of five seats, those seats will reliably represent the left, center and right of every district—resulting in a truly representative Congress.

This year's elections put a spotlight on the troubled nature of how we elect the House of Representatives, the alleged "people's house." But some of our smartest election experts don't seem to understand the root of the problems with House elections. More importantly, they fail to communicate that it's simply impossible to address those problems within the straightjacket of single-member district, winner-take-all elections.

As one example, take Attorney General Eric Holder's otherwise laudable speech in Boston on December 11th on the subject of expanding and upholding the right to vote. Holder said, "We should consider reforms to the redistricting process for state and federal offices—so districts are drawn in a way that's neutral, that promotes fair and effective representation for all, and that can't be abused to protect incumbents and undercut electoral competition."

That sounds wonderful, as does the implication in a December 15th *New York Times* news story about problems in US House elections that independent redistricting would result in House elections accurately reflecting voter preference. In fact, it's an utter illusion to expect that the adoption of independent redistricting could come close to achieving the seven values that we believe any fair electoral system should promote: accountable leadership, responsive government, electoral competition, geographically coherent districts, fair representation of racial diversity, fair representation of women, and fair opportunities for everyone to cast meaningful votes in every election. In fact, it's unlikely that any redistricting plan can achieve more than two of these seven objectives.

But there is a way to accomplish all seven goals with just one electoral reform: passing statutes to enact fair voting proposals for congressional elections. It's time for analysts to confront the implications of this reality if we want our country to move toward a representative democracy fit for the 21st century.

In this analysis we will focus on the problem of winner-take-all elections through the lens of US House races, but transformative change may come sooner to our state legislatures. They are easier to reform through ballot measures and tend to be even less representative than Congress. Most state legislative chambers are run by one party for decades at a time, if not centuries. Incumbents are often even more cushioned from electoral accountability, with two out of five state legislative races won in uncontested races this year. Such dominance and lack of competition is primarily grounded in winner-take-all elections, not gerrymandering.

Let's start our review of House elections with the simple premise that elections should uphold majority rule. This year, the outcome of the elections defied that principle. Democratic congressional candidates won the most votes in US House races, but Republicans won 33 more House seats. Remarkable examples of distorted outcomes include Republicans in North Carolina and Pennsylvania winning 22 of 31 seats despite losing the popular vote in both states.

Whole regions were dominated by one party. Democrats won all 21 US House races in New England, while Republicans won all 22 congressional districts in the line of states stretching from Arkansas to Idaho. Most congressional races across the country were no-choice landslides, with more than 63% of races won by at least 20% or not contested at all. Women's representation increased by only 1%, leaving men again with more than four in five House seats despite the once-in-a-decade opportunity for winning in new seats triggered by redistricting. The already-shrunken caucus of House moderates saw its numbers sharply reduced yet again to levels far short of its support among voters.

Deeply disturbing as they may be, most of these problems aren't new. Congressional elections have distorted fair representation and marginalized most voters for decades. But the rising dominance of partisanship in governing how people vote has locked down election outcomes more than at any time in the modern era. Structural inequalities have been brought to the fore, including the basic fact of allowing a party to control the House after being defeated at the polls.

The Biased House

Democrats had a very good 2012 election. In the presidential race, Barack Obama defeated Mitt Romney by 126 electoral votes and nearly five million popular votes. Republicans won only eight Senate races, the worst performance for a major party in Senate races since the 1950s.

In House races, Democratic candidates won about a million more votes nationwide than Republicans. After controlling for factors like vote inflation for incumbents and uncontested races, the data suggests voters generally preferred Democrats for Congress by a 52%–48% margin, underscored by the fact that not a single Democrat lost in the 181 most Democratic districts.

And despite widespread popular concern about Congress being too polarized, losing incumbents came heavily from the moderate wings of both parties.

Yet Republicans won a comfortable majority of 234 to 201 seats. That disparity in voter preference compared to seats did not result from ticket-splitting; in fact, there were only 24 districts in which one party's nominee carried the presidential vote and the other party's nominee won the congressional race, all but four of which were won by an incumbent. The real problem for Democrats was that in a year in which Barack Obama won a decisive presidential election victory, he apparently has carried only 207 of 435 congressional districts.

The results were so incongruous that many commentators have identified structure as the likely explanation. We welcome attention to structure, given that the centrality of its role is too often overlooked in explaining election outcomes and parties' policy preferences. In this case, however, the great majority of analysts utterly missed the real story. Again and again, they suggested that the problem was the Republican-controlled redistricting process in 2011–2012. By naming the wrong cause of the distorted election results, they miss what is most in need of reform.

Among many examples of this line of thinking, the Daily Kos identified redistricting as the reason for the Republican victory "pure and simple." Mother Jones published a much-shared investigative report that suggested Republicans won because "they drew the lines." Think Progress described Republican gerrymandering as "a simple explanation for how this happened." Slate published an article called "How Ridiculous Gerrymanders Saved the House Republican Majority." The Brennan Center touted the use of independent redistricting as the way to ensure "ordinary citizens [have] their voices heard."

All of those claims are, at best, highly misleading. They're not wrong that partisan gerrymandering is a problem—it is, as FairVote has argued for years—but in suggesting that gerrymandering is sufficient to explain why the Democrats unjustly lost the House this year, why Congress is so dysfunctional and why most Americans live in no-choice congressional districts.

The distortion between voter intent and outcome and the reduction of centrist legislators has relatively little to do with how redistricting was done in 2011 compared *with the very fact of districting itself.* One of the people to get that part of the story right was Hendrik Hertzberg in a must-read commentary in the *New Yorker.* Hertzberg wrote:

> Gerrymandering routinely gets blamed for such mismatches, but that's only part of the story. Far more important than redistricting is just plain districting: because so many Democrats are city folk, large numbers of Democratic votes pile up redundantly in overwhelmingly one-sided districts.

To be sure, Republicans certainly benefitted from redistricting, as FairVote demonstrated in its analysis this summer. They controlled the redistricting process in many large states, and won several more seats this year than they would have otherwise as a result.

But the Republican victory in the 2012 House elections isn't explained by the relatively few seats they gained through gerrymandering. Although 52% of voters at the polls had an underlying preference for Democrats, Democrats won only 46% of seats. As a result, Republicans won fully 25 more seats than they would have if the outcome had been reflective of voter preference.

Nor can gerrymandering explain the dramatic collapse of congressional moderates, who typically are Members elected in districts leaning toward the other major party. With only 10 members set to represent districts that favor the opposing party by more than 52% to 48%, the nation's substantial bloc of centrist voters will be even more woefully underrepresented than Democrats.

There was another factor at play, almost entirely ignored by most pundits. It is the real root of the representation problem in our country and could be changed by a simple federal statute: winner-take-all elections. That fact may seem inconvenient or disruptive to how people think about our democracy, but it can no longer be seriously disputed. It's time to stop living in a world of delusion about how our elections work.

The Case for a Natural Demographic Structural Bias

The idea that recent Republican gerrymandering alone caused the 25-seat Republican distortion is discredited by a simple look at district partisanship. There are currently 241 districts in which Barack Obama underperformed his national average in 2008. Before redistricting, there were 232 such districts. A report by the Brennan Center similarly showed a gain of 11 districts favoring Republicans compared to 2010. Further quantitative analysis from political science professors writing for the Monkey Cage reached similar conclusions.

Changes in districts alone clearly don't explain the partisan imbalance, although they did exacerbate it. Another partial explanation is the effect of incumbency. Because incumbents usually have the advantages of greater name recognition and greater funds, they tend to get a boost of a few percentage points over challengers—what FairVote calls "the incumbency bump." Since there were more Republican incumbents running than Democrats in 2012, it makes sense that Republicans would win a few more seats than Democrats even in a neutral year with unbiased districts.

But incumbency only goes so far. Take a very recent counterexample: the 2010 elections, in which Democrats had an even greater incumbency advantage than the one enjoyed by Republicans in 2012, as 230 Democratic incumbents ran for re-election in 2010. Needless to say, that advantage did not save the Democrats from losing control of the House by a wide margin.

[...]

Furthermore, if only gerrymandering and incumbents were to blame for the 2012 Republican victory, there would not be so much compelling evidence of a Republican congressional bias even before the 2000 and 2010 redistrictings. In 2000, for example, George Bush lost the national popular vote by more than a half million votes, but carried 21 more House districts than Al Gore, as detailed in FairVote's 2011 report *Fuzzy Math*. FairVote's first *Monopoly Politics* report in 1997 also showed a stark Republican bias in a decade in which Democrats had largely controlled redistricting. Democrats held most state legislatures during the redistricting process that followed the 1990 census, but in 1996 there were 239 districts leaning toward Republicans and only 196 toward Democrats.

Gerrymandering and incumbency are not sufficient to explain the extent of the Republican House victory in 2012. The problem runs deeper for Democrats—and all Americans who believe in the importance of leadership that is electorally accountable to their constituents and risks being booted out if voters perceive that they have failed to do their job. We have that accountability in races for governor and, to a lesser extent due to antiquated rules governing the Electoral College, the presidential race. But it's lacking in elections for Congress and most of our state legislatures.

A Brief History of the Structurally Lopsided House

With most voters responding either positively or negatively to the presidency of Barack Obama in 2010, the congressional elections that year marked a distinct increase in partisan voting behavior, as evidenced by how Republicans' congressional election success was confined nearly entirely to districts leaning toward their party. The election exposed a fundamental partisan bias that has existed, relatively unnoticed, for decades.

[...]

The sharp decline in the number of candidates able to win in the other party's turf is also the key reason for the dwindling number of centrist representatives. Members of Congress are much more likely to vote moderately when representing a district favoring the opposing party rather than one favoring their own, even narrowly. In 2012, four Democratic incumbents lost against non-incumbents—all of them in strongly Republican-leaning districts. On the Republican side, nine incumbents lost among the 17 Democratic-leaning districts they held going into the election, but only seven incumbents lost among the 173 districts they had held with a Republican lean.

[...]

Independent Redistricting Has Value, But Not for Fairness in Representation

Once identifying partisan redistricting as the main problem in House elections, analysts inevitably focus on just one structural solution: converting to more independent redistricting processes along the lines of Iowa's criteria-driven rules or California's independent redistricting commission. Nonpartisan and bipartisan redistricting commissions are already used to some degree in nine states with more than one district, and often represent a positive change for the redistricting process by making it far harder for partisans to help their political friends and hurt their political enemies. But they do little to resolve the partisan bias in House elections, are often not trusted by racial minorities concerned about upholding voting rights, and do little to promote balanced representation of the left, right and center in Congress.

Analysts such as those at Fells Stats have made the assumption that nationwide independent redistricting commissions would produce purely proportional results. That assumption would only hold true if a commission's first and dominant priority was to create districts that accurately represented the partisanship of the state as a whole. In theory, it is possible to draw district lines that would always create a House that accurately reflects the will of the American people, but only through "reverse gerrymanders" that would spread urban voters out into suburban and rural areas. Those maps end up with districts looking like the spokes of a wheel, as in the incredible congressional gerrymander conjured by Democrats in Maryland in 2011.

Independent redistricting committees don't actually operate that way, and few of their adherents envision such gerrymanders as part of the solution, as so much of their rhetoric targets bizarre-looking districts. As an example of how commissions really work,

Arizona's independent commission lists the following criteria for drawing its districts, in rough order of priority:

- Equal population
- Compactness and contiguousness
- Compliance with the US Constitution and the Voting Rights Act
- Respect for communities of interest
- Incorporation of visible geographic features, including city, town and county boundaries, as well as undivided census tracts
- Creation of competitive districts where there is no significant detriment to other goals

Accurately representing the partisan popular vote of the state is not even listed as a criterion, much less a priority. Nor is it likely to be a key consideration as long as we continue to place importance on values like compactness, contiguousness, and incorporation of city borders and geographic features—and districts drawn without consideration of these factors would essentially defeat the purpose of having representatives for specific geographic districts in the first place.

The 2012 elections show the futility of relying on independent redistricting committees to provide voter choice and fair representation in the House. [...] You simply can't gerrymander the nation into solely 50-50 districts—and even if you could do so, fair representation would be unlikely.

It's no surprise, then, that independent redistricting commissions prioritize factors other than creating competitive districts when drawing their maps. The prevalence of largely noncompetitive districts and the structural bias against Democrats in the House will persist even if independent commissions are implemented nationwide. The difficulty faced by Democrats— and, more broadly, by urban and suburban voters—is shown clearly by red-blue partisan maps of the nation by county and congressional district based on the 2012 election. They demonstrate that drawing compact districts would leave the Democratic vote under-represented in the House because of its concentration relative to Republicans.

Romney defeated Obama in nearly four of every five counties. Those county successes translate into congressional seat wins for the Republican Party when representation in House elections is determined more by where you live than what you think. Seeing how winner-take-all dominance crosses state lines makes it clear that redistricting tends to only reflect partisan imbalance, not create it. It is the combination of winner-take-all elections, single-member districts, and partisan polarization that is the root cause of our distorted representation and lopsided outcomes in the House.

The Only Route to Balancing Congress: Constitutional Forms of Fair Voting

The real problem at the root of the Democratic demographic disadvantage is the statutory decision to elect House Members exclusively through single-seat, winner-take-all elections. Democratic candidates win by huge margins in many urban and suburban districts, while Republicans win by smaller but still very safe margins in many more districts. The differences are stark. Democrats represent 47 districts with a partisanship or more than 70% to 30% in their favor, while Republicans represent only 23 such districts. Of the 16 districts with a partisan split of at least 80%-20%, Democrats represent 15.

The best way to remove the structural unfairness inherent in the current House of Representatives is to get rid of winner-take-all elections. FairVote has a plan to do just that, grounded in our Constitution and American electoral traditions. The first requirement is an act of Congress. The more ambitious plan would be for Congress to prohibit winner-take-all elections in all states that elect more than one House Member. A more modest step would be to repeal the congressional mandate for states to use single-member districts that was established in a 1967 law.

[…]

Choice voting is a ranked choice system in which like-minded voters who make up 20% of a district would be sure of electing a candidate to at least one of five seats. It would reliably result in balanced and accurate representation of the left, center and right of every district, as would several other proven voting methods that are consistent with our traditions of voting for candidates rather than for parties.

[...]

As a result, fair voting plans for the US Congress would make every "super district" competitive, with all voters able to participate in congressional elections that would not be predetermined by district partisanship. Both Democrats in Republican districts and Republicans in Democratic districts who are now essentially disenfranchised by winner-take-all elections would have real chances to help elect a representative. In fact, every single super district would likely elect at least one Republican and one Democrat in our plan, with a more representative mix of voices elected within the parties as well as between them.

Representation would broaden in other ways as well. Independents and third parties would have a real chance to hold the major parties accountable, better reflecting the rising number of voters who choose to register to vote as independents or outside the two party structure.

[...]

Fair voting and multi-member districts are fully constitutional. For the first half-century of congressional elections, at least one state—and usually many more—elected House members in statewide elections. The movement to single-member districts was ironically driven by the goal of partisan fairness, avoiding distortions from the use of statewide winner-take-all elections. We know today from the experiences of fair voting systems at a local level, in Illinois state legislative elections and in most democracies around the world, that fair voting methods provide a far more reliable means of accomplishing that goal.

We should expand that local and state use of fair voting. But we also shouldn't let Congress off the hook: the "people's house" demands an electoral system that truly represents the people.

Conclusion: Avoiding the "Gerrymandering Is the Problem" Trap

Make no mistake—there is one predominant reason why the Democrats lost the House in 2012 and why so many seats are lopsided: winner-take-all elections in single-member districts. Independent redistricting commissions would help mitigate the problem of unfair dominance of congressional elections by one party, but the underlying GOP tilt would remain. Unless winner-take-all is ended, Democrats will continue to suffer from a system that is fundamentally rigged against them. All voters will suffer from voting in noncompetitive districts, not being able to hold their Members or congressional leadership accountable, and not having the ability to earn nuanced political representation beyond the poles of the two parties.

It's time for a real change in American congressional elections—and for that, Democrats and Republicans who want to compete in all corners of the country should join with all underrepresented Americans to identify the true cause of the problems with our House elections. It only stokes the growing partisan divide to take the easy way out and put the blame on the opposing party. The real enemy isn't particular parties or personalities, but our decision to keep winner-take-all rules in place that let 51% of voters determine 100% of the representation.

Winner-take-all elections divide us rather than bring us together. To get every American on the same side, we need to reject winner-take-all and promote shared representation, competitive choice and more accountable leadership by adopting fair voting systems of proportional representation.

Organizations to Contact

The editors have compiled the following list of organizations concerned with the issues debated in this book. The descriptions are derived from materials provided by the organizations. All have publications or information available for interested readers. The list was compiled on the date of publication of the present volume; the information provided here may change. Be aware that many organizations take several weeks or longer to respond to inquiries, so allow as much time as possible.

All About Redistricting
Loyola Law School
919 Albany Street
Los Angeles, CA 90015
(213) 736-1000
email: justin.levitt@lls.edu
website: redistricting.lls.edu

Professor Justin Levitt of Loyola Law School tracks state and local redistricting efforts as well as court cases about gerrymandering. He provides charts, maps, and other graphics to explain the trends in gerrymandering legislation on a state and national level. Readers can also find resources on the website to help them better understand the existing districts and the redistricting process.

American Civil Liberties Union
125 Broad Street, 18th Floor
New York, NY 10004
(212) 549-2500
email: www.aclu.org/secure/report-lgbthiv-discrimination
website: www.aclu.org

The ACLU is a nationwide nonprofit organization with over one million members that works to defend and preserve the individual rights and liberties guaranteed by the Constitution and laws of the United States. It works to change policy by lobbying the federal Congress and state houses to pass bills that advance or defend civil liberties. The organization also files lawsuits on behalf of those who have had their civil rights violated, with some cases being argued before the Supreme Court.

The Brennan Center for Justice
120 Broadway, Suite 1750
New York, NY 10271
(646) 292-8310
email: brennancenter@nyu.edu
website: www.brennancenter.org

The Brennan Center for Justice at NYU School of Law is a nonpartisan law and policy institute that pushes for transparency and justice in our political system. It works to hold political institutions and laws accountable for upholding the ideals of democracy through fighting for Constitutional protection in Congress, state legislatures, and the courts.

Fair Districts PA
226 Forster Street
Harrisburg, PA 17102
(800) 313-1597
website: www.fairdistrictspa.com

Fair Districts PA is a nonpartisan, citizen-led, statewide coalition working to create a process for redistricting that is transparent, impartial, and fair in the state of Pennsylvania. Ultimately the organization aims to have the Pennsylvania Constitution amended to replace the current partisan redistricting process with an independent, impartial Citizens Redistricting Committee.

The Fair Elections Legal Network
1825 K Street NW, Suite 450
Washington, DC 20006
(202) 331-0114
email: info@fairelectionsnetwork.com
website: www.FairElectionsNetwork.com

The Fair Elections Legal Network (FELN) is a national nonpartisan organization focused on voting rights, legal support, and election reform. Its mission is to remove barriers to registration and voting for traditionally underrepresented constituencies. The organization aims for improved election administration through administrative, legal, and legislative reform. It provides free legal advice and representation to voter mobilization organizations.

FairVote
6930 Carroll Avenue, Suite 240
Takoma Park, MD 20912
(301) 270-4616
email: info@fairvote.org
website: www.fairvote.org

FairVote is a nonpartisan champion of electoral reforms that give voters greater choice, a stronger voice, and a representative democracy that works for all Americans. It works for electoral reforms on the local, state, and national level through research and greater communication. The organization's website provides access to its research and offers information on the electoral process.

HeadCount
104 West 29th Street, 11th Floor
New York, NY 10001
(866) OUR-VOTE.
email: info@headcount.org
website: headcount.org

HeadCount is a nonpartisan organization that works to empower Americans through voter registration, digital campaigns, information, and projects that harness the power of music and culture. It seeks to inform artists and fans about the issues and assist them in registering to vote in the hopes of creating a politically influential force.

The National Democratic Redistricting Committee
email: info@democraticredistricting.com.
website: https://democraticredistricting.com

The National Democratic Redistricting Committee is chaired by the 82nd attorney general of the United States Eric H. Holder Jr. and supported by former president Barack Obama. It offers a four-part strategy for defeating gerrymandering: advancing legal action, mobilizing grassroots campaigns, supporting reforms, and winning targeted elections.

Project Vote
1420 K Street NW, Suite 700
Washington, DC 20005
(202) 546-4173
email: info@projectvote.org
website: http://www.projectvote.org

Project Vote is a national, nonpartisan nonprofit organization founded on the belief that an organized, diverse electorate is the key to a better America. The organization has primarily focused on improving voter registration, with goals to eliminate disparities in registration rates between minorities and majorities, encourage state governments to play a leading role in voter registration, and ensure that constituency-based organizations have the resources they need to run effective voter registration drives. Members engage in advocacy, litigation, and technical assistance to achieve these goals.

Rock the Vote
1875 Connecticut Avenue NW, 10th Floor
Washington, DC 20009
(866) OUR-VOTE
email: info@rockthevote.com
website: www.rockthevote.org

Rock the Vote is a nonpartisan nonprofit organization dedicated to building the political power of young people. It focuses on using pop culture, music, art, and technology to engage young people in politics. The organization provides information on voter registration, elections, and voting rights.

Bibliography

Books

Charles S. Bullock III, *Redistricting: The Most Political Activity in America*. Lanham, MD: Rowman & Littlefield, 2010.

David T. Canon, *Race, Redistricting, and Representation: The Unintended Consequences of Black Majority Districts*. Chicago, IL: University of Chicago Press, 1999.

Jay K. Dow, *Electing the House: The Adoption and Performance of the U.S. Single-Member District Electoral System*. Wichita, KA: University Press of Kansas, 2017.

Philip Kotler, *Democracy in Decline: Rebuilding Its Future*. Thousand Oaks, CA: SAGE, 2016.

Gordon Lafer, *The One Percent Solution: How Corporations Are Remaking America One State at a Time*. Ithaca, NY: Cornell University Press, 2017.

David Lublin, *The Paradox of Representation*. Princeton, NJ: Princeton University Press, 1999.

Jane Mayer, *Dark Money: The Hidden History of the Billionaires Behind the Rise of the Radical Right*. New York, NY: Anchor, 2017.

Anthony J. McGann, Charles Anthony Smith, Michael Latner, and Alex Keena, *Gerrymandering in America: The House of Representatives, the Supreme Court, and the Future of Popular Sovereignty*. New York, NY: Cambridge University Press, 2016.

Nicholas R. Seabrook, *Drawing the Lines: Constraints on Partisan Gerrymandering in U.S. Politics*. Ithaca, NY: Cornell University Press, 2017.

Jonathan Winburn, *The Realities of Redistricting: Following the Rules and Limiting Gerrymandering in State Legislative Redistricting*. Lanham, MD: Lexington, 2009.

Periodicals and Internet Sources

Alvin Chang, "How the Supreme Court Could Limit Gerrymandering, Explained with a Simple Diagram," Vox, October 9, 2017. https://www.vox.com/policy-and -politics/2017/10/9/16432358/gerrymandering-supreme -court-diagram.

Nate Cohn and Quoctrung Bui, "How the New Math of Gerrymandering Works," *New York Times*, October 3, 2017. https://www.nytimes.com/interactive/2017/10/03/upshot /how-the-new-math-of-gerrymandering-works-supreme -court.html.

Christopher Ingraham, "America's most gerrymandered congressional districts," *The Washington Post*, May 15, 2014, https://www.washingtonpost.com/news/ wonk/wp/2014/05/15/americas-most-gerrymandered- congressional-districts/?utm_term=.87ed535f2954

Christopher Ingraham, "This Is the Best Explanation of Gerrymandering You Will Ever See," *Washington Post*, March 1, 2015. https://www.washingtonpost .com/news/wonk/wp/2015/03/01/this-is-the-best -explanation-of-gerrymandering-you-will-ever-see/?utm_ term=.6f04a033d04f.

Brian Klaas, "Gerrymandering Is the Biggest Obstacle to Genuine Democracy in the United States. So Why Is No One Protesting?" *Washington Post*, February 10, 2017. https://www.washingtonpost.com/news/democracy-post /wp/2017/02/10/gerrymandering-is-the-biggest-obstacle -to-genuine-democracy-in-the-united-states-so-why-is-no -one-protesting/?utm_term=.fdf446175c63.

Laura Moser, "This Is How Gerrymandering Works," *New York Review of Books*, December 18, 2017. http://www.nybooks .com/daily/2017/12/18/this-is-how-gerrymandering-works.

Vann R. Newkirk II, "The Supreme Court Finds North Carolina's Racial Gerrymandering Unconstitutional," *Atlantic*, May 22, 2017. https://www.theatlantic .com/politics/archive/2017/05/north-carolina -gerrymandering/527592.

Mike Pearl, "The Texas Gerrymandering Trial Could Change All of America," Vice, July 16, 2017. https://www.vice.com /en_nz/article/kzanm3/the-texas-gerrymandering-trial -could-change-all-of-america.

Olivia Walch, "Changing the Math on Gerrymandering: What Would a Proper Congressional District Look Like?" The Nib, October 5, 2017. https://thenib.com/changing-the -math-on-gerrymandering.

Sam Wang, "The Great Gerrymander of 2012," *New York Times Review of Books*, February 2, 2013. http://www.nytimes .com/2013/02/03/opinion/sunday/the-great-gerrymander -of-2012.html?pagewanted=all.

Index

Fourteenth Amendment, 42,
43, 102, 103, 105

G

Gaddie, Keith, 59, 60, 62
Gerry, Elbridge, 59, 65–66, 98
gerrymandering
  aims and tactics of, 7–8, 31–34
  derivation of term, 59, 65–66,
    98
  effect on voters, 14–16, 97–98
  and efficiency gap, 25–30, 35,
    38, 43
  explanation of, 7, 11–24, 31,
    65–68, 98
  legal cases, 8, 9, 13, 18–19,
    19–20, 21, 26–28, 31,
    32, 33, 34, 37, 38, 41–45,
    58–64, 67, 69–76, 99–111
  prison-based gerrymandering,
    77–81
  racial gerrymandering, 8, 31,
    32, 69–76, 99–111
Gillette, Greg, 31–34
Gill v. Whitford, 9, 26–27, 28,
  41–42, 43–44, 45
Ginsburg, Ruth Bader, 18–19
Giuliani, Rudy, 107
Gonzalez, Charles A., 73
Gorsuch, Neil, 41
Green, Al, 73
Green Party, 82–96
gridlocking, 65, 67–68
Griffith, Thomas B., 71, 73
Grofman, Bernard, 108

H

Helms, Jesse, 104–105, 106
Hertzberg, Hendrik, 117
Holder, Eric, 113–114

I

instant runoff voting, 90–91

J

Johnson, Eddie Bernice, 73

K

Katzenbach, Nicholas, 106
Keating, Frank, 63
Kennedy, Anthony, 59, 103
Kennedy, Liz, 11–24
Kousser, J. Morgan, 108

L

Lee, Sheila Jackson, 73
Lee, Suevon, 69–76
Lublin, David, 109

M

majoritarian election method,
  48, 49, 50
majority-minority district,
  explanation of, 8
Marchant, Kenny, 74
McCain, John, 56, 63
McCarty, Nolan, 62
Mehaji, Jais, 52–57
Miller v. Johnson, 105, 106